C++
Pocket Reference

C++
Pocket Reference

Kyle Loudon

O'REILLY®

Beijing · Cambridge · Farnham · Köln · Sebastopol · Taipei · Tokyo

C++ Pocket Reference

by Kyle Loudon

Copyright © 2003 O'Reilly Media, Inc. All rights reserved.
Printed in Canada.

Published by O'Reilly Media, Inc., 1005 Gravenstein Highway North, Sebastopol, CA 95472.

O'Reilly Media, Inc. books may be purchased for educational, business, or sales promotional use. Online editions are also available for most titles (*safari.oreilly.com*). For more information, contact our corporate/institutional sales department: (800) 998-9938 or *corporate@oreilly.com*.

Editor:	Jonathan Gennick
Production Editor:	Emily Quill
Cover Designer:	Ellie Volckhausen
Interior Designer:	David Futato

Printing History:

May 2003:	First Edition.

ISBN: 978-0-596-00496-5
[T]

Contents

Introduction   1
    Typographic Conventions   2
    Acknowledgments   2
    Compatibility with C   2

Program Structure   3
    Startup   3
    Termination   5
    Header Files   5
    Source Files   7
    Preprocessor Directives   8
    Preprocessor Macros   11

Fundamental Types   12
    bool   12
    char and wchar_t   13
    short, int, long   15
    float, double, long double   16

Compound Types   17
    Enumerations   18
    Arrays   19
    Strings   22
    Pointers   24
    Pointers to Members   26

References 27
Class Types 28

Type Conversions and Definitions **28**
Type Conversions 28
Type Definitions 31

Lexical Elements **31**
Comments 32
Identifiers 32
Reserved Words 33
Literals 34
Operators 34
Expressions 46

Scope **47**
Local Scope 47
Class Scope 47
Namespace Scope 48
File Scope 48
Other Scopes 49
Enclosing Scopes 49

Declarations **50**
Declaring Variables 51
Declaring Functions 52
Storage Classes 55
Qualifiers 57

Statements **59**
Expression Statements 59
Null Statements 59
Compound Statements 59
Iteration Statements 60

Selection Statements	62
Jump Statements	64

Namespaces | **66**
using Declarations	67
using Directives	67
Unnamed Namespaces	68

Classes, Structs, and Unions | **68**
Declaring Objects	69
Accessing Members	69
Declaring Data Members	70
Declaring Member Functions	74
Access Levels for Members	78
Friends	79
Constructors	80
Destructors	83
Nested Declarations	85
Forward Declarations	86
Structs	86
Unions	86

Inheritance | **88**
Constructors and Inheritance	89
Destructors and Inheritance	90
Virtual Member Functions	91
Abstract Base Classes	94
Access Levels for Inheritance	94
Multiple Inheritance	95
Virtual Base Classes	97

Templates | **98**
| Template Classes | 98 |
| Template Functions | 101 |

Overloading   **104**

Overloading Functions   104

Overloading Operators   105

Memory Management   **108**

Memory Allocation   108

Memory Reclamation   110

Casts and Runtime Type Information   **112**

C-Style Casts   112

Casts in C++   112

Runtime Type Information   115

Exception Handling   **117**

try   117

throw   117

catch   118

Exception Specifications   119

The C++ Standard Library   **120**

The std Namespace   121

C Standard Library Support   121

C++ Standard Header Files   122

I/O Streams   122

C++ Pocket Reference

Introduction

The *C++ Pocket Reference* is a quick reference to the C++ programming language as defined by the international standard *INCITS/ISO/IEC 14882–1998*. It consists of a number of short sections, each further divided into specific topics. Many of the topics include pointed, canonical examples.

At the outset, it is important to recognize that C++ is a vast language, admittedly difficult to describe in a pocket reference. As a result, this reference is devoted almost exclusively to presenting the language itself. Other references are available from O'Reilly & Associates describing the C++ Standard Library, a vast subject on its own. The C++ Standard Library includes all of the facilities of the C Standard Library plus many new ones, such as the Standard Template Library (STL) and I/O streams.

This book has been written for developers with a variety of backgrounds and experience levels in C++. Those with experience using C++ will find this book to be a uniquely focused reference to its most commonly used features. If you are new to C++, you may wish to work with a tutorial first and return to this reference later to research specific topics.

Typographic Conventions

This book uses the following typographic conventions:

Italic
> This style is used for filenames and for items emphasized in the text.

`Constant width`
> This style is used for code, commands, keywords, and names for types, variables, functions, and classes.

`Constant width italic`
> This style is used for items that you need to replace.

Acknowledgments

I would like to thank Jonathan Gennick, my editor at O'Reilly, for his support and direction with this book. Thanks also to Uwe Schnitker, Danny Kalev, and Ron Passerini for taking the time to read and comment on an early draft of this book.

Compatibility with C

With some minor exceptions, C++ was developed as an extension, or superset, of C. This means that well-written C programs generally will compile and run as C++ programs. (Most incompatibilities stem from the stricter type checking that C++ provides.) So, C++ programs tend to look syntactically similar to C and use much of C's original functionality.

This being said, don't let the similarities between C and C++ fool you into thinking that C++ is merely a trivial derivation of C. In fact, it is a rich language that extends C with some grand additions. These include support for object-oriented programming, generic programming using templates, namespaces, inline functions, operator and function overloading, better facilities for memory management, references, safer forms of casting, runtime type information, exception handling, and an extended standard library.

Program Structure

At the highest level, a C++ program is composed of one or more *source files* that contain C++ source code. Together, these files define exactly one starting point, and perhaps various points at which to end.

C++ source files frequently import, or *include*, additional source code from *header files*. The C++ preprocessor is responsible for including code from these files before each file is compiled. At the same time, the preprocessor can also perform various other operations through the use of *preprocessor directives*. A source file after preprocessing has been completed is called a *translation unit*.

Startup

The function main is the designated start of a C++ program, which you as the developer must define. In its standard form, this function accepts zero or two arguments supplied by the operating system when the program starts, although many C++ implementations allow additional parameters. Its return type is int. For example:

```
int main( )
int main(int argc, char *argv[])
```

argc is the number of arguments specified on the command line; argv is an array of null-terminated (C-style) strings containing the arguments in the order they appear. The name of the executable is stored in argv[0], and may or may not be prefixed by its path. The value of argv[argc] is 0.

The following shows the main function for a simple C++ program that prompts the user for actions to perform on an account:

```
#include <iostream>
#include <cmath>
#include <cstdlib>
using namespace std;
```

```cpp
#include "Account.h"

int main(int argc, char *argv[])
{
   Account       account(0.0);
   char          action;
   double        amount;

   if (argc > 1)
      account.deposit(atof(argv[1]));

   while (true)
   {
      cout << "Balance is "
           << account.getBalance()
           << endl;

      cout << "Enter d, w, or q: ";
      cin >> action;

      switch (action)
      {
         case 'd':
            cout << "Enter deposit: ";
            cin >> amount;
            account.deposit(amount);
            break;

         case 'w':
            cout << "Enter withdrawal: ";
            cin >> amount;
            account.withdraw(amount);
            break;

         case 'q':
            exit(0);

         default:
            cout << "Bad command" << endl;
      }
   }

   return 0;
}
```

The class for the account is defined in a later example. An initial deposit is made into the account using an amount specified on the command line when the program is started. The function `atof` (from the C++ Standard Library) is used to convert the command-line argument from a string to a `double`.

Termination

A C++ program terminates when you return from `main`. The value you return is passed back to the operating system and becomes the return value for the executable. If no return is present in `main`, an implicit return of 0 takes places after falling through the body of `main`. You can also terminate a program by calling the `exit` function (from the C++ Standard Library), which accepts the return value for the executable as an argument.

Header Files

Header files contain source code to be included in multiple files. They usually have a *.h* extension. Anything to be included in multiple places belongs in a header file. A header file should never contain the following:

- Definitions for variables and static data members (see "Declarations" for the difference between declarations and definitions).
- Definitions for functions, except those defined as template functions or inline functions.
- Namespaces that are unnamed.

NOTE

Header files in the C++ Standard Library do not use the *.h* extension; they have no extension.

Often you create one header file for each major class that you define. For example, Account is defined in the header file *Account.h*, shown below. Of course, header files are used for other purposes, and not all class definitions need to be in header files (e.g., helper classes are defined simply within the source file in which they will be used).

```
#ifndef ACCOUNT_H
#define ACCOUNT_H

class Account
{
public:
                Account(double b);

    void        deposit(double amt);
    void        withdraw(double amt);
    double      getBalance() const;

private:
    double      balance;
};

#endif
```

The implementation of this class is in *Account.cpp*. You use the preprocessor directive #include to include a header file within another file (see "Preprocessor Directives").

Because header files are often included by other headers themselves, care must be taken not to include the same file more than once, which can lead to compilation errors. To avoid this, it is conventional to wrap the contents of header files with the preprocessor directives #ifndef, #define, and #endif, as done in the previous example.

The tactic of wrapping a header file forces the preprocessor to test an identifier. If that identifier is not defined, the preprocessor defines it and processes the file's contents. As an example, the contents of *Account.h* are processed only when ACCOUNT_H is undefined, and the first thing that processing does is to define ACCOUNT_H to ensure the header is not processed a second time. To ensure uniqueness, *X_H* is typically used as the identifier, where *X* is the name of the header file without its extension.

Source Files

C++ source files contain C++ source code. They usually have a *.cpp* extension. During compilation, the compiler typically translates source files into object files, which often have a *.obj* or *.o* extension. Object files are joined by the linker to produce a final executable or library.

Often you create one source file for each major class you implement. For example, the implementation of Account is in *Account.cpp*, shown below. Of course, there is no requirement about this; source files often contain more than just the implementation of a single class.

```cpp
#include "Account.h"

Account::Account(double b)
{
    balance = b;
}

void Account::deposit(double amt)
{
    balance += amt;
}

void Account::withdraw(double amt)
{
    balance -= amt;
}

double Account::getBalance() const
{
    return balance;
}
```

Preprocessor Directives

The C++ preprocessor can be used to perform a number of useful operations controlled via several directives. Each directive begins with a pound sign (#) as the first character that is not whitespace on a line. Directives can span multiple lines by including a backslash (\) at the end of intermediate lines.

#define

The #define directive replaces an identifier with the text that follows it wherever the identifier occurs in a source file. For example:

```
#define         BUFFER_SIZE 80

char            buffer[BUFFER_SIZE];
```

If you specify no text after the identifier, the preprocessor simply defines the identifier so that any check for its definition tests true and it expands to nothing in the source code. (You can see this in use earlier where ACCOUNT_H was defined.)

NOTE

In C++, it is preferable to use enumerations, and to a lesser degree, variables and data members declared using the keywords const or static const for constant data, rather than the #define directive.

The #define directive can accept arguments for macro substitution in the text. For example:

```
#define MIN(a, b) (((a) < (b)) ? (a):(b))

int             x = 5, y = 10, z;

z = MIN(x, y);    // This sets z to 5.
```

In order to avoid unexpected problems with operator precedence, parameters should be fully parenthesized in the text, as shown above.

In C++, it is preferable to use templates and inline functions in place of macros. Templates and inline functions eliminate unexpected results produced by macros, such as MIN(x++, y) incrementing x twice when a is less than b. (Macro substitution treats x++, not the result of x++, as the first parameter.)

#undef

The #undef directive undefines an identifier so that a check for its definition tests false. For example:

```
#undef LOGGING_ENABLED
```

#ifdef, #ifndef, #else, #endif

You use the #ifdef, #ifndef, #else, and #endif directives together. The #ifdef directive causes the preprocessor to include different code based on whether or not an identifier is defined. For example:

```
#ifdef LOGGING_ENABLED
cout << "Logging is enabled" << endl;
#else
cout << "Logging is disabled" << endl;
#endif
```

Using #else is optional. #ifndef works similarly but includes the code following the #ifndef directive only if the identifier is not defined.

#if, #elif, #else, #endif

The #if, #elif, #else, and #endif directives, like the directives of #ifdef, are used together. These cause the preprocessor to include or exclude code based on whether an expression is true. For example:

```
#if (LOGGING_LEVEL == LOGGING_MIN && \
    LOGGING_FLAG)
cout << "Logging is minimal" << endl;
```

```
#elif (LOGGING_LEVEL == LOGGING_MAX && \
    LOGGING_FLAG)
cout << "Logging is maximum" << endl;
#elif LOGGING_FLAG
cout << "Logging is standard" << endl;
#endif
```

The #elif (else-if) directive is used to chain a series of tests together, as shown above.

#include

The #include directive causes the preprocessor to include another file, usually a header file. You enclose standard header files with angle brackets, and user-defined header files with quotes. For example:

```
#include <iostream>
#include "Account.h"
```

The preprocessor searches different paths depending on the form of enclosure. The paths searched depend on the system.

#error

The #error directive causes compilation to stop and a specified string to be displayed. For example:

```
#ifdef LOGGING_ENABLED
#error Logging should not be enabled
#endif
```

#line

The #line directive causes the preprocessor to change the current line number stored internally by the compiler during compilation in the macro __LINE__. For example:

```
#line 100
```

A filename optionally can be specified in double quotes after the line number. This changes the name of the file stored internally by the compiler in the macro __FILE__. For example:

```
#line 100 "NewName.cpp"
```

#pragma

Some operations that the preprocessor can perform are implementation-specific. The #pragma directive allows you to control these operations by specifying the directive along with any parameters in a form that the directive requires. For example:

```
#ifdef LOGGING_ENABLED
#pragma message("Logging enabled")
#endif
```

Under Microsoft Visual C++ 6.0, the message directive informs the preprocessor to display a message during compilation at the point where this line is encountered. The directive requires one parameter: the message to display. This is enclosed in parentheses and quoted.

Preprocessor Macros

The C++ preprocessor defines several macros for inserting information into a source file during compilation. Each macro begins and ends with two underscores, except for _ _cplusplus, which has no terminating underscores.

_ _LINE_ _
> Expands to the current line number of the source file being compiled.

_ _FILE_ _
> Expands to the name of the source file being compiled.

_ _DATE_ _
> Expands to the date on which the compilation is taking place.

_ _TIME_ _
> Expands to the time at which the compilation is taking place.

_ _TIMESTAMP_ _
> Expands to the date and time at which the compilation is taking place.

__STDC__

> Will be defined if the compiler is in full compliance with the ANSI C standard.

__cplusplus

> Will be defined if the program being compiled is a C++ program. How a compiler determines whether a given program is a C++ program is compiler-specific. You may need to set a compiler option, or your compiler may look at the source file's extension.

Fundamental Types

The type for an identifier determines what you are allowed to do with it. You associate a type with an identifier when you declare it. When declaring an identifier, you also may have the opportunity to specify a storage class and one or more qualifiers (see "Declarations").

The fundamental types of C++ are its Boolean, character, integer, floating-point, and void types. The Boolean, character, and integer types of C++ are called *integral types*. Integral and floating-point types are collectively called *arithmetic types*.

bool

Booleans are of type bool. The bool type is used for values of truth. For example:

```
bool             flag;
...
if (flag)
{
    // Do something when the flag is true.
}
```

Boolean values

Booleans have only two possible values: true or false. The typical size of a bool is one byte.

Boolean literals

The only Boolean literals are the C++ keywords `true` and `false`. By convention, false is defined as 0; any other value is considered true.

char and wchar_t

Characters are of type `char` or `wchar_t`. The `char` type is used for integers that refer to characters in a character set (usually ASCII). For example:

```
char            c = 'a';

cout << "Letter a: " << c << endl;
```

The `wchar_t` type is a distinct type large enough to represent the character sets of all locales supported by the implementation. To use facilities related to the `wchar_t` type, you include the standard header file *<cwchar>*.

Character types may be specified either as `signed` or `unsigned` and are sometimes used simply to store small integers. For example:

```
signed char     small = -128;
unsigned char   flags = 0x7f;
```

A `signed char` represents both positive and negative values, typically by sacrificing one bit to store a sign. An `unsigned char` doesn't have a sign and therefore can hold larger positive values, typically twice as large. If neither `signed` nor `unsigned` is specified, characters are usually signed by default, but this is left up to the compiler.

Character values

The range of values that characters may represent is found in the standard header file *<climits>*. The size of a char is one byte. The size of a byte technically is implementation-defined, but it is rarely anything but eight bits. The size of the wchar_t type is also implementation-defined, but is typically two bytes.

Character literals

Character literals are enclosed by single quotes. For example:

```
char            c = 'A';
```

To specify literals for wide characters, you use the prefix L. For example:

```
wchar_t         c = L'A';
```

To allow special characters, such as newlines and single quotes, to be used within literals, C++ defines a number of *escape sequences*, each of which begins with a backslash. Table 1 presents these escape sequences. There is no limit to the number of hexadecimal digits that can appear after \x in a hexadecimal escape sequence. Octal escape sequences can be at most three digits.

Table 1. Character escape sequences

Escape sequence	Description
\a	Alert (system bell)
\b	Backspace
\f	Form feed
\n	Newline
\r	Carriage return
\t	Horizontal tab
\v	Vertical tab
\\	Backslash
\'	Single quote
\"	Double quote
\?	Question mark
ooo	Octal number *ooo*
\x*hhh*...	Hexadecimal number *hhh*...

short, int, long

Integers are of type short, int, or long. These types differ in size and the range of values they can represent. For example:

```
short       sval = 32767;
int         ival = 2147483647;
long        lval = 0x7fffffff;
```

Integers may be specified as either signed or unsigned. For example:

```
signed short       total;
unsigned short     flags = 0xf0f0;
```

Signed integers represent both positive and negative values, typically by sacrificing one bit to store a sign. Unsigned integers don't have a sign and therefore can hold larger positive values. If an integer is not specified as either signed or unsigned, it is signed by default.

Integer values

The range of values that each of the integer types may represent is found in the standard header file *<climits>*. The exact size of a short, int, or long is left up to the compiler, but is typically two, four, or four bytes respectively. Although the size of each type can vary, the compiler guarantees that the size of a short is less than or equal to the size of an int, and the size of an int is less than or equal to the size of a long.

Integer literals

Literals for integers have several forms, as shown in Table 2. If U, u, L, or l is not used as a suffix, the compiler assigns a type appropriate for the magnitude of the literal.

Table 2. Integer literals

Examples	Description
12 -5	The most common form of integer literals.
012 0377	Literals that begin with 0 are octal values (e.g., 012 is the octal literal for the decimal number 10).
0x2a 0xffff	Literals that begin with 0x are hexadecimal values (e.g., 0x2a is the hexadecimal literal for the decimal number 42).
256L 0x7fL	Literals with L (or l) in the suffix are treated as long.
0x80U 0xffffUL	Literals with U (or u) in the suffix are treated as unsigned.

float, double, long double

Floating points are of type float, double, or long double. These types differ in size and in the range and precision of values they can represent. For example:

```
float       fval = 3.4e+38F;
double      dval = 1.7e+308;
```

Floating-point values

The range and precision of values that each of the floating-point types may represent is found in the standard header file *<cfloat>*. The exact size, range, and precision of a float, double, or long double is left up to the compiler, but is typically four, eight, or ten bytes respectively. Although the size of each type can vary, the compiler guarantees that the size of a float is less than or equal to the size of a double, and the size of a double is less than or equal to the size of a long double.

Floating-point literals

Literals for floating points can take on several forms, as shown in Table 3. If F, f, L, or l is not used as a suffix, the compiler assigns a type of double.

Table 3. Floating-point literals

Examples	Description
1.2345 -57.0 0.4567	The most common form of literal floating points.
1.992e+2 1.71e-25	Literals expressed in scientific notation.
8.00275F 3.4e+38L	Literals with the suffix F (or f) are given the type float; literals with the suffix L (or l) are given the type long double.

void

The void type indicates the absence of a value. One use is in declaring functions that do not return a value. For example:

```
void sayHello( )
{
    cout << "Hello" << endl;
}
```

Another use is in declaring a pointer that can point to any type of data. For example:

```
int             i = 200;
void            *p = &i;
```

The variable p points to an int. Variables that are not pointers cannot be declared as void.

Compound Types

Arithmetic types are the building blocks for more complex types, called *compound types*. These include enumerations, arrays, strings, pointers, pointers to members, references, and the various class types of C++, as well as functions. Arithmetic types, enumerations, pointers, and pointers to members are collectively called *scalar types*.

Enumerations

An enumeration, specified by the keyword enum, is a set of integer constants associated with identifiers, called *enumerators*, that you define. In general, enumerations provide a way to use meaningful names where you might otherwise use integer constants, perhaps defined using the preprocessor directive #define. Enumerations are preferred over the preprocessor for this in C++ because they obey the language's rules of scope. The following defines an enumeration for the colors of the rainbow:

```
enum SpectrumColor
{
                Red,    Orange, Yellow,
                Green,  Blue,   Indigo,
                Violet
};
```

If you plan to instantiate variables to store values of an enumeration, you can give the enumeration a name (here, SpectrumColor); however, a name is not required. With this enumeration, you can write a loop to cycle through the colors of the rainbow, for example:

```
for SpectrumColor operator++(SpectrumColor &s, int dummy)
{
    return s = (s >= Violet) ? Red : SpectrumColor(s + 1);
}
```

Following are some additional points to keep in mind about enumerations:

- You can specify values for enumerators within an enumeration, which you can then use in place of integer constants.

- When you let the compiler assign values to enumerators, it assigns the next integer after the one assigned to the preceding enumerator.

- Values start at 0 if you do not provide a value for the first enumerator.

- You can use enumerators anywhere that you would use an int.
- You cannot assign arbitrary integers to a variable of an enumeration type.
- The size of integers for enumerations is no larger than the size of an int, unless a larger integer is needed for explicit values.

The following example illustrates these points:

```
enum
{
                ASCII_NUL,      // 0
                ASCII_SOH,      // 1
                ASCII_STX,      // 2

                ASCII_A = 65,   // 65
                ASCII_B,        // 66

                BufferSize = 8  // 8
};

char            buffer[BufferSize];
```

Arrays

Arrays contain a specific number of elements of a particular type. So that the compiler can reserve the required amount of space when the program is compiled, you must specify the type and number of elements that the array will contain when it is defined. The compiler must be able to determine this value when the program is compiled. For example:

```
enum
{
                HandleCount = 100
};

int             handles[HandleCount];
```

Once an array has been defined, you use the identifier for the array along with an index to access specific elements within the array. The following sets each element in the previous array to an initial value of −1:

```
for (int i = 0; i < HandleCount; i++)
{
    handles[i] = -1;
}
```

Arrays are zero-indexed; that is, the first element is at index 0. This indexing scheme is indicative of the close relationship in C++ between pointers and arrays and the rules that the language defines for pointer arithmetic. In short, the assignment in the example above is equivalent to the following:

```
*(handles + i) = -1;
```

It is important to remember that no bounds-checking is performed for arrays.

Multidimensional arrays

C++ supports multidimensional arrays, which are arrays defined using more than one index, as follows:

```
enum
{
                Size1 = 4,
                Size2 = 4
};

double          matrix[Size1][Size2];
```

Arrays can be defined with more than two indices in a similar manner. Once a multidimensional array is defined, you use multiple indices to access a specific element, as follows:

```
for (int i = 0; i < Size1; i++)
    for (int j = 0; j < Size2; j++)
        matrix[i][j] = 0.0;
```

The relationship between pointers and arrays extends to multidimensional arrays as well. In short, the assignment in the example above is equivalent to the following:

```
*(*(matrix + i) + j) = 0.0;
```

Passing arrays to functions

When defining a function that has an array as a parameter, all but the first dimension must be specified for the parameter. This ensures that the proper pointer arithmetic can be performed. In the case of an array with a single dimension, this means that no dimension is required:

```
void f(int handles[])
{
    handle[0] = 0;
}
```

In the case of an array with two dimensions, for example, the second dimension must be specified:

```
void g(double matrix[][Size2])
{
    matrix[0][Size2 - 1] = 1.0;
}
```

You can also define equivalent functions that use pointer parameters:

```
void f(int *handles)
{
    handles[0] = 0;
}

void g(double (*matrix)[Size2])
{
    matrix[0][Size2 - 1] = 1.0;
}
```

The parentheses are needed in the second case so that the array is a multidimensional array of double values, not a one-dimensional array of double pointers.

Initializer lists for arrays

An initializer list for an array is a comma-delimited list of values by which to initialize the array's elements. The list is enclosed by braces ({}). Each value's type must be acceptable for the type of elements that the array has been declared to contain. For example:

```
enum SwitchState
{
                On, Off
};

SwitchState    switches[] =
               {
                 On, Off, On, Off
               };
```

When you initialize an array with an initializer list, you may omit the array size in the declaration; enough space will be allocated for the array to accommodate the values specified. If you provide a size but specify values for fewer elements than the size indicates, the missing elements are default-initialized. The rules for default initialization are complicated; you should not rely on them.

Initializer lists can also be used to initialize arrays that are multidimensional. The rules are essentially the same as for arrays of one dimension, except that an initializer list for a multidimensional array uses nested braces to align its values in a manner consistent with the size of each dimension.

```
char           tictactoe[3][3] =
               {
                 {'_', '_', '_',},
                 {'_', '_', '_',},
                 {'_', '_', '_'}
               };
```

Strings

Character (C-style) strings are arrays of characters terminated with a null character (\0). The characters of the string are of type char, or type wchar_t for wide-character strings. For example:

```
enum
{
                NameLength = 81
};
```

```
char             name[NameLength];
wchar_t          wide[NameLength];
```

You must allocate one extra character for the null terminator in arrays of characters to be used for strings. Functions that return a string's length, such as strlen (from the C++ Standard Library), do not include a string's null terminator in the length returned. Wide-character versions of standard facilities typically have the prefix w or use wcs instead of str (e.g., wostream, wcsncpy, etc.).

NOTE

Although many facilities in the C++ Standard Library work with character (C-style) strings, the preferred way to work with strings in C++ is to use the string class from the C++ Standard Library. The wide-character version is wstring.

String literals

String literals are enclosed in double quotes. For example:

```
char             name[] = "Margot";
```

Long string literals can be broken into quoted strings separated by whitespace for style, when needed. For example:

```
char             s[] = "This string is "
                       "on two lines.";
```

To specify literals for wide-character strings, you use the prefix L. For example:

```
wchar_t          wide[] = L"Margot";
```

The compiler allocates enough space for a string, including its null terminator. An empty string ("") actually has space reserved for one character: the null terminator. The storage for a string literal is guaranteed to exist for the life of the program, even for a string literal defined locally within a block. The type of a string literal is an array of const char or wchar_t elements of static duration.

Pointers

For any type *T*, there is a corresponding type *pointer to T* for variables that contain addresses in memory of where data of type *T* resides. *T* is the *base type* of a pointer to *T*. Pointers are declared by placing an asterisk (*) before the variable name in a declaration (see "Declaring Variables"). In the following example, i is an int while *iptr is a pointer to i:

```
int             i = 20;
int             *iptr = &i;
```

Normally you can set a pointer of a specific type only to the address of data of that same type, as just shown. However, in the case of a pointer to a class, the pointer can also be assigned the address of an object of some type derived from that class. This is essential for polymorphism (see "Virtual Member Functions"). For example, if Circle were derived from Shape (see "Inheritance"), we could do the following:

```
Circle          c;
Shape           *s = &c;
```

Pointer dereferencing

Dereferencing a pointer yields what the pointer points to. To dereference a pointer, you precede it with an asterisk in an expression, as shown in the commented lines below:

```
int             i = 20;
int             *iptr = &i;
int             j;
int             k = 50;

j = *iptr;      // This sets j to i.
*iptr = k;      // This sets i to k;
```

Pointer arithmetic

Pointers in expressions are evaluated using the rules of *pointer arithmetic*. When an operator for addition, subtraction, increment, or decrement is applied to a pointer *p* of type *T*, *p* is treated as an array of type *T*. As a result, *p + n* points to the *n*th successive element in the array, and $p - n$ points to the *n*th previous element. If *n* is 0, $p + n$ points to the first element in the array. So, if *T* were a type with a size of 24 bytes, p += 2 would actually increase the address stored in *p* by 48 bytes.

Pointer arithmetic illustrates the close relationship between pointers and arrays in C++. However, pointers and arrays do have a fundamental difference: whereas a pointer can be modified to point to something else, an array cannot be changed to point away from the data it was created to reference.

Void pointers

Pointers of type void are permitted to point to data of any type. For example:

```
Circle          c(2.0);
void            *p;

p = &c;         // c is a circle.
```

When assigning a void pointer to a pointer of some other type, an explicit cast is required. For example:

```
Circle          *c;

c = static_cast<Circle *>(p);
```

Void pointers cannot be dereferenced or used with pointer arithmetic.

Null pointers

Pointers of any type can be assigned the value 0, which indicates that the pointer points to nothing at all. A pointer with the value 0 is called a *null pointer*. You should never dereference a null pointer.

Function pointers

A function pointer is a pointer that points to a function. Its type is related to the signature of the function to which it points. For example, the following defines a function named addOne, then defines inc as a pointer to a function that takes a reference to an int as a parameter and returns void. inc is then set to addOne, which has that same signature:

```
void addOne(int &x)
{
    x += 1;
}

void          (*inc)(int &x) = addOne;
```

The last line could also be written as shown below (using the address-of operator, &, before addOne):

```
void          (*inc)(int &x) = &addOne;
```

Parentheses are needed around inc so that the asterisk is associated with the name of the pointer, not the type. Once a function pointer points to a function, it can be used to invoke the function, as follows:

```
int           a = 10;

inc(a);       // This adds 1 to a.
```

The last line could also be written as shown below (using the indirection operator, *, before the pointer):

```
(*inc)(a);
```

Pointers to Members

Pointers to members are like alternative names for class members (see "Classes, Structs, and Unions"). For example, assume that class X has a member of type int called data:

```
int           X::*p = &X::data;
X             object;
X             *objptr = new X;

int           i = object.*p;
int           j = objptr->*p;
```

This sets i to the value of data in object, and j to the value of data in the object addressed by objptr.

References

References are used to provide alternative names for variables. They are declared by placing an ampersand (&) before the variable name in a declaration. For example:

```
int         i = 20;
int         &r = i;
```

Because a reference always has to refer to something, references must be initialized where they are defined. Therefore, a reasonable way to think of a reference is as a constant pointer. Once initialized, the reference itself cannot be made to refer to anything else; however, the variable or object to which it refers can be modified. Operations applied to the reference affect the variable or object to which the reference refers. For example:

```
int         i = 20;
int         &r = i;

r++;        // This increments i.
```

Normally you can set a reference of a specific type to a variable of that same type, as just shown. However, in the case of a reference to a class, the reference can also refer to an object of some type derived from that class. Therefore, like pointers, references support polymorphic behavior (see "Virtual Member Functions"). For example, if Circle were derived from Shape (see "Inheritance"), you could do the following:

```
Circle      c;
Shape       &s = c;
```

Reference parameters

A common use of references is with parameters for functions. References allow changes to parameters to be reflected in the caller's environment. For example:

```
void xchg(int &x, int &y)
{
    int t = x;
    x = y;
    y = t;
}
```

Using the definition above, you could swap two integers a and b by doing the following:

```
xchg(a, b);
```

If x and y were not references in the definition of xchg, the contents of x and y would be swapped within the function, but the contents of a and b would be unchanged when the function returned.

References as l-values

References are also often used in C++ as return values for functions. This allows the return value of a function to be used as an *l-value*, which is a value that can appear on the left side of an assignment.

Class Types

The class types of C++ are classes, structs, and unions (see "Classes, Structs, and Unions").

Type Conversions and Definitions

In C++ you can convert a value of one type into a value of another type. Such an action is called a *type conversion*. You can also define your own type names using the typedef keyword.

Type Conversions

Type conversions are performed when you use a cast explicitly (see "Casts and Runtime Type Information"), and at times implicitly by the compiler. For example, the compiler converts a type implicitly when the types in a binary operation are not the same. A compilation error occurs if no conversion is possible.

Implicit conversions

Implicit conversions occur between C++'s arithmetic types, between certain pointer types (see "Pointers"), and between user-defined types and others. The implicit conversion of arithmetic types and pointer types in binary operations is carried out by converting the smaller or less precise type to the larger or more precise one. Booleans, characters, and integers smaller than an int are first converted to an int using *integral promotion*. When an integer and a floating point appear in the same operation, the integer is converted to the floating-point type.

Preservation of values

The implicit conversion of arithmetic types is performed in such a way as to preserve the original values of the entities being converted whenever possible. However, there are many situations in which surprising results can occur. For example, a compiler may not warn about conversions from wider or more precise types to smaller or less precise ones (e.g., from long to short, or double to float), in which a wider value may not be representable in the smaller type. In addition, the conversion from an unsigned type to a signed one can result in a loss of information.

User-defined conversions

You can specify explicit conversions for user-defined types by defining user-defined conversion operators (see "Overloading Operators"). For example, the following user-defined conversion operator, operator double, converts an Account object to a double:

```
class Account
{
public:
```

```
                    Account(double b)
                    {
                        balance = b;
                    }

                    operator double()
                    {
                        return balance;
                    }
    ...
    private:
        double          balance;
    };
```

This user-defined conversion operator allows you to use a value of type Account where you might otherwise use a double:

```
    Account         account(100.0);
    double          balance = account;
```

When C++ sees the assignment of an Account value to a double variable, it invokes operator double to perform the conversion.

Converting constructors

A constructor that has a single parameter and is not declared using explicit can be used by the compiler to perform implicit conversions between the type of the parameter and the class type. For example:

```
    class Account
    {
    public:
                    Account(double b)
                    {
                        balance = b;
                    }
    ...
    private:
        double          balance;
    };
```

The constructor in this class allows you to do the following, for example:

```
    Account         account = 100.0;
```

Type Definitions

Frequently it is useful to provide an alternative name for types that have long or otherwise unwieldy names. This is accomplished using typedef.

To define a new name for a type, you use the keyword typedef followed by the old type, then the new type. The following example defines uint32 to mean unsigned long:

```
typedef unsigned long uint32;

uint32          value32bit;
```

This illustrates using typedef to define your own sized-integer type (e.g., int8, int16, int32, etc.). Some compilers define __int8, __int16, and so forth; typedef provides a way to use types like these with any compiler. Another common use of typedef is in providing alternative names for parameterized types, which tend to be long, when working with the Standard Template Library. For example:

```
typedef map<int, string> IntStringMap;

IntStringMap    m;
```

Lexical Elements

At the most fundamental level, a C++ program consists of individual lexical elements called *tokens*. Tokens are delineated by whitespace (spaces, newlines, tabs, etc.), or can be formed once the start of another token is recognized, as shown below:

```
ival+3
```

This stream actually consists of three tokens even though there is no whitespace. The tokens are ival, +, and 3. In the absence of whitespace, the compiler forms tokens by consuming the longest possible token as it scans from left to right.

Tokens are passed to the parser, which determines if a stream of tokens has the correct syntax. Tokens together form more complex semantic constructs, such as declarations, expressions, and statements that affect the flow of execution.

Comments

Comments are notes written in the source code for developers; they are ignored completely by the compiler. The preprocessor converts each comment to a single space before the compiler ever gets the chance to see it.

A comment is any block of text enclosed between /* and */, or following // on a single line. Comments of the first form cannot be nested within one another. They usually span multiple lines. For example:

```
/* This comment has more than one line.
   Here is another part of the comment.*/
```

Comments of the second form are useful for short explanations that do not occupy more than a single line. For example:

```
z = MIN(x, y);     // z is the smallest.
```

Once a single-line comment begins, it occupies the remainder of the line. There is no way to end the comment before this.

Identifiers

Identifiers in C++ are sequences of characters that are used for names of variables, functions, parameters, types, labels, namespaces, and preprocessor macros. Identifiers may consist of letters, digits, and underscores, but they must not begin with a digit. For example, the following are all legal C++ identifiers:

```
i           addressBook     Mgr         item_count
ptr2        NAME_LENGTH     class_       showWindow
```

The following rules apply to identifiers:

- Identifiers are case-sensitive, and they must not be one of the C++ reserved words (see "Reserved Words").

- Identifiers that begin with an underscore are reserved for implementations of the language.

- Although C++ imposes no limit on the size of identifiers, your compiler and linker will have size limits that you should consider in practice.

NOTE

There is no one stylistic convention for identifiers upon which everyone agrees. One common convention, however, is to use lowercase characters to begin names for local variables, data members, and functions. Uppercase characters are then used to begin the names of types, namespaces, and global variables. Names processed by the preprocessor are written entirely in uppercase. Names of parameters in macros are written entirely in lowercase.

Reserved Words

C++ defines a number of keywords and alternative tokens, which are sequences of characters that have special meaning in the language. These are reserved words and cannot be used for identifiers. The reserved words of C++ are listed below:

and	and_eq	asm
auto	bitand	bitor
bool	break	case
catch	char	class
compl	const	const_cast
continue	default	delete
do	double	dynamic_cast
else	enum	explicit
export	extern	false
float	for	friend
goto	if	inline

int	long	mutable
namespace	new	not
not_eq	operator	or
or_eq	private	protected
public	register	reinterpret_cast
return	short	signed
sizeof	static	static_cast
struct	switch	template
this	throw	true
try	typedef	typeid
typename	union	unsigned
using	virtual	void
volatile	wchar_t	while
xor	xor_eq	

Literals

Literals are lexical elements that represent explicit values in a program. C++ defines many types of literals. Each is described under its respective type in "Fundamental Types."

Operators

An operator is used to perform a specific operation on a set of operands in an expression. Operators in C++ work with anywhere from one to three operands, depending on the operator.

Associativity

Operators may associate to the left or right. For example, assignment operators (=, +=, <<=, etc.) associate to the right. Therefore, the following:

```
i = j = k
```

actually implies:

```
i = (j = k)
```

On the other hand, the operator for addition (+) associates to the left. Therefore, the following:

```
i + j + k
```

actually implies:

```
(i + j) + k
```

Precedence

Operators also have an order, or *precedence*, by which expressions that contain them are evaluated. Expressions containing operators with a higher precedence are evaluated before those containing operators with a lower precedence.

You can use parentheses around an expression to force grouping. Even when not essential, it's best to use parentheses in expressions to document your intentions. The number of operators in C++ often makes their precedence difficult to remember.

Table 4 lists the operators of C++ from highest precedence to lowest and describes how each operator associates. Each section contains operators of equal precedence. The table also describes the behavior of each operator when used with the intrinsic types of C++. For most operators, C++ lets you define additional behaviors for your own types (see "Overloading Operators").

Table 4. Operators

Operator	Description	Associates
::	Scope resolution	No
[]	Array subscript	Left
.	Member selection	Left
->	Member selection	Left
( )	Function call	Left
( )	Value construction	No
++	Postfix increment	No
--	Postfix decrement	No
typeid	Type information	No
*_cast	C++ cast	No

Table 4. Operators (continued)

Operator	Description	Associates
sizeof	Size information	No
++	Prefix increment	No
--	Prefix decrement	No
~	Bitwise NOT	No
!	Logical NOT	No
-	Unary minus	No
+	Unary plus	No
&	Address-of	No
*	Indirection	No
new	Allocate	No
new[]	Allocate	No
delete	Deallocate	No
delete[]	Deallocate	No
( )	C-style cast	Right
.*	Pointer-to-member selection	Left
->*	Pointer-to-member selection	Left
*	Multiply	Left
/	Divide	Left
%	Modulo (remainder)	Left
+	Add	Left
-	Subtract	Left
<<	Shift left	Left
>>	Shift right	Left
<	Less than	Left
<=	Less than or equal to	Left
>	Greater than	Left
>=	Greater than or equal to	Left
==	Equal to	Left
!=	Not equal to	Left

Table 4. Operators (continued)

Operator	Description	Associates
&	Bitwise AND	Left
^	Bitwise XOR	Left
|	Bitwise OR	Left
&&	Logical AND	Left
||	Logical OR	Left
? :	Conditional expression	Right
=	Simple assignment	Right
*=	Multiply and assign	Right
/=	Divide and assign	Right
%=	Modulo and assign	Right
+=	Add and assign	Right
-=	Subtract and assign	Right
<<=	Shift left and assign	Right
>>=	Shift right and assign	Right
&=	AND and assign	Right
^=	XOR and assign	Right
|=	OR and assign	Right
throw	Throw exception	Right
,	Sequence	Left

Additional information about the behaviors of the operators in C++ is summarized in the following sections.

Scope resolution (::)

The scope resolution operator is used to specify a scope (see "Scope"). For example, the following invokes a static member function of a class called `Dialog`:

```
dialog = Dialog::createDialog( );
```

The scope operator can also be used without a scope name to specify file (global) scope. For example:

```
::serialize(i);
```

This ensures that the global function serialize is invoked, even if serialize has been declared within the local scope.

Array subscript ([ ])

The array subscript operator is used to access individual elements of arrays or memory referenced by pointers. For example:

```
tmp = table[0];
```

This assigns the first element in an array called table to tmp. The expression between the brackets indicates the element.

Member selection (. and ->)

Member selection operators are used to specify members of objects (see "Classes, Structs, and Unions"). You use the dot form with objects and the arrow form with pointers to objects. For example:

```
object.f();
```

This invokes member function f of an object called object. The following illustrates the arrow form:

```
objptr->f();
```

This invokes member function f for an object that is addressed by the pointer objptr.

Function call (())

The function call operator, which is ( ), is used to invoke a function. For example:

```
f(a, b);
```

This invokes a function called f with two arguments, a and b.

Value construction (())

The value construction operator, which is also ( ), is used to create an instance of a type. For example:

```
g(Circle(5.0));
```

This constructs a temporary object that is an instance of the Circle class, which is passed to g.

Postfix increment and decrement (++, −−)

The postfix increment and decrement operators increment or decrement an operand, but the value of the operand within its expression is the value prior to modification. For example:

```
void count( )
{
   static int    i = 0;

   if (i++ == 0)
   {
      // This is the first time called.
   }
}
```

The value of i prior to being incremented is tested for equality with 0. Because i is initialized to 0, the test is true during the first invocation of the function.

typeid

The typeid operator gets runtime type information for an operand. See "Casts and Runtime Type Information" for a complete description of this operator.

C++ cast

Type cast operators specific to C++ are dynamic_cast, static_cast, const_cast, and reinterpret_cast. See "Casts and Runtime Type Information" for a complete description of these operators.

sizeof

The sizeof operator gets the size of its operand. For example:

```
size_t          s = sizeof(c);
```

This initializes s to the size of c. The operand may be an expression or type. The result is an integer of type size_t.

Prefix increment and decrement (++, −−)

The prefix increment and decrement operators increment or decrement an operand. The value of the operand within its expression is the value after modification. For example:

```
void count( )
{
   static int    i = 0;

   if (++i == 1)
   {
      // This is the first time called.
   }
}
```

The value of i after being incremented is tested for equality with 1. Because i is initialized to 0, the test is true during the first invocation of the function.

Bitwise NOT (~)

The bitwise NOT operator computes the bitwise complement of its operand. For example:

```
unsigned char   bits = 0x0;
bits = ~bits;
```

This assigns 0xFF back into bits, assuming a character is eight bits. The operand must be one of the Boolean, character, or integer types of C++.

Logical NOT (!)

The logical NOT operator reverses the truth of its operand; it yields false if its operand is true (nonzero) and true if its operand is false. For example:

```
bool            done = false;

while (!done)
{
    // Set done to true when finished.
}
```

This loop is repeated until something in the loop sets done to true. The result of the logical NOT operator is a bool.

Unary minus and plus (−, +)

The unary minus and plus operators compute the negative and positive values their operands. For example:

```
i = -125;
j = +273;
```

Because the unary plus operator simply returns the value of its operand (promoted to an int), it is seldom used.

Address-of (&)

The address-of operator gets the address at which its operand resides in memory. For example:

```
Circle          c;
Circle          *p = &c;
```

This assigns the address of c to the Circle pointer p. The address is a pointer derived from the type of the operand.

Indirection (*)

The indirection operator dereferences a pointer and gets the value that it addresses. For example:

```
int             i;
int             *p = new int;

*p = 5;
i = *p;
```

This assigns the value 5 to i. The type of the result is the type from which the pointer is derived. The operand must be a pointer.

Allocate and deallocate

The C++ memory management operators are new, new[], delete, and delete[]. They allocate and reclaim memory on the heap. See "Memory Management" for a complete description of these operators.

C-style cast (())

The C-style cast operator converts the type of its operand to a new type (see "C-Style Casts"). For example:

```
void              *p = new int;
*p = 10;
int               *q = (int *)p;
```

This casts p from a void pointer to an int pointer. No run-time checking is performed to ensure that the cast is legal.

Pointer-to-member selection (.* and –>*)

The .* and ->* operators access a class member via a pointer to the member. For example:

```
int               X::*p = &X::data;
X                 object;
X                 *objptr = new X;

int               i = object.*p;
int               j = objptr->*p;
```

This sets i to the value of data in object, and j to the value of data in the object addressed by objptr. You use the dot form with objects and the arrow form with pointers to objects.

Arithmetic (*, /, %, +, –)

Arithmetic operators perform multiplication (*), division (/), modulus (%), addition (+), and subtraction (–) using two operands. For example:

```
if (x % 2 == 0)
{
   // The integer x is an even number.
}
```

The modulo operator computes the remainder of dividing the first operand by the second. For example, if dividing an integer by 2 has no remainder, the integer is even.

Shift left and right (<<, >>)

The shift operators shift bits to the left (<<) or right (>>). For example:

```
unsigned char   bits = 0x1;
bits = bits << 2;
```

This assigns 0x4 back into bits. The first operand is the one shifted; the second is the number of bits to shift. Both operands must be one of the Boolean, character, or integer types of C++. These operators are commonly used for insertion and extraction with I/O streams as well (see "I/O Streams").

Relational (<, <=, >, >=, ==, !=)

Relational operators compare two operands, yielding true if the comparison is true and false if the comparison is false. For example:

```
for (int i = 0; i < 100; i++)
{
    // Do something for each iteration.
}
```

This loop uses the less-than operator to determine when to stop looping. The result of using a relational operator is a bool.

Bitwise AND, XOR, and OR (&, ^, |)

The bitwise AND (&), XOR (^), and OR (|) operators perform bitwise operations. Each bit in the first operand is compared with the same bit in the second. For the bitwise AND operator, if both bits are 1, the corresponding result bit is 1; otherwise, the bit is 0. For example, the following sets a to 0x0F:

```
unsigned char   a, b = 0x0f, c = 0xff;
a = b & c;
```

For the bitwise XOR operator, if one bit is 0 and the other is 1, the corresponding result bit is 1; otherwise, the bit is 0. For example, the following sets a to 0xA0:

```
unsigned char     a, b = 0xaa, c = 0x0a;
a = b ^ c;
```

For the bitwise OR operator, if both bits are 0, the corresponding result bit is 0; otherwise, the bit is 1. For example, the following sets a to 0x0F.

```
unsigned char     a, b = 0x0f, c = 0x0a;
a = b | c;
```

The operands of these bitwise operators must both be one of the Boolean, character, or integer types of C++.

Logical AND and OR (&&, ||)

The logical AND (&&) and OR (||) operators combine two operands to evaluate their truth. The logical AND operator yields true only if both operands are true (nonzero); otherwise, it yields false. Both conditions in the following example must be true in order to execute the block containing the comment:

```
int               i = 10;
int               *p = &i;

if (p != NULL && *p < 100)
{
    // Do something if both are true.
}
```

The logical OR operator yields true if either operand is true; otherwise, it yields false. For example:

```
bool              doneWithTask1 = false;
bool              doneWithTask2 = false;

while (!doneWithTask1 || !doneWithTask2)
{
    // One of the tasks has not finished.
}
```

Either condition can be true for the block containing the comment to be executed.

For both operators, if a result can be determined from the first operand alone, the second operand is not evaluated. When these operators are overloaded, both operands are always evaluated.

Conditional expression (?:)

The conditional expression operator uses the value of one operand to determine whether to evaluate the second or third operand. For example:

```
i = (p != NULL) ? *p : -1;
```

If the first operand is true, the result is the second operand; otherwise, the result is the third. The first operand appears before the question mark (?); the second and third operands are separated by a colon (:).

Simple and compound assignments
(=, *=, /=, %=, +=, -=, <<=, >>=, &=, |=, ^=)

Assignment operators assign the value of one operand to another. For example:

```
i = (j + 10) * 5;
```

This is the simplest form of assignment; the second operand is simply evaluated and stored into the first. The other assignment operators perform compound assignments. For example:

```
i += 5;
```

This adds 5 to i and assigns the result back to i. Therefore, it has the same effect as the following but avoids the need for i to be evaluated twice:

```
i = i + 5;
```

After any assignment, the value of the expression is the value that was assigned. This allows assignments to be chained together, as follows:

```
a = b = c;
```

Exception (throw)

The throw operator is used to throw an exception. See "Exception Handling" for a complete description of this operator.

Sequence (,)

The sequence operator, which is a comma, evaluates two operands from left to right. The value of the expression becomes the value of the last operand. For example:

```
for (i = 0, j = 10; i < 10; i++, j--)
{
    // Increase i while making j smaller.
}
```

In this case, the result of i=0, j=10 is 10. However, both assignments are performed; both variables are initialized.

Expressions

An expression is something that yields a value. Nearly every type of statement uses an expression in some way. For example, the declaration below uses an expression for its initializer:

```
int             t = (100 + 50) / 2;
```

The simplest expressions in C++ are just literals or variables by themselves. For example:

```
1.23     false     "string"     total
```

More interesting expressions are formed by combining literals, variables, and the return values of functions with various operators to produce new values. These can then be used in expressions themselves. For example, the following are all C++ expressions:

```
i->getValue() + 10
p * pow(1.0 + rate,(double)mos))
new char[20]
sizeof(int) + sizeof(double) + 1
```

Scope

A name can be used only within certain regions of a program. These regions define its *scope*. The scope of a name is based on where, and to some extent how, you declare it. Most names have one of four scopes. Labels and prototype parameters have their own special scopes.

Local Scope

A name has local scope when it is declared inside of a block. A block is a compound statement that begins with a left brace ({) and ends with a right brace (}). For example:

```
void f( )
{
   int          i = 10;
   ...
}
```

In this example, i has local scope. A name with local scope is visible only within its block.

Class Scope

A name has class scope when it is declared within the confines of a class and does not have local scope. For example:

```
class Event
{
public:
   enum Type
   {
                keyDown,
                ...
   };
   ...
   Type          getType( ) const
                {
                    return type;
                }
   ...
private:
```

```
    Type            type;
    ...
};
```

Here, Type, keyDown, getType, and type all have class scope. A name with class scope is visible inside of the class in which it is declared, and outside of the class using a selection or scope operator, depending on what the name represents. To use a name with class scope outside of its declaring class, the access level for the name must also allow access to it (see "Access Levels for Members").

NOTE

A name declared within a block that is within a class has a scope local to that block, and does not have class scope.

Namespace Scope

A name declared inside of a namespace has namespace scope (see "Namespaces"). For example:

```
namespace Aviation
{
    const double    NMPerSM = 0.826201;
}
```

This places NMPerSM, used for converting nautical to statute miles, in a namespace called Aviation. A name with namespace scope is visible inside of the namespace in which it is declared, and outside of the namespace with the scope operator.

File Scope

A name that is not declared in a block, class, or namespace has file scope. A name with file scope can be used anywhere within a file after the point where the name is declared. A name for a variable, object, or function with file scope that has not been declared using the keyword static is called a

---

global. This is because it can be used potentially anywhere in a program.

Other Scopes

Labels (see "Jump Statements") and the parameters in prototypes have their own scopes. The scope of a label is the function in which the label is used, even if the label is defined inside of a block. This allows jumping into or out of a block. The scope of a prototype parameter goes to the end of the prototype; however, a parameter cannot be used to define default values for other parameters.

Enclosing Scopes

A name is visible in any scope that its declaring scope encloses. For example:

```
const double      NMPerSM = 0.826201;

double convertToSM(double nm)
{
    return nm * NMPerSM;
}
```

Since the local scope of convertToSM is enclosed by the file scope in which NMPerSM is declared, NMPerSM is visible within convertToSM.

A name declared in one scope *hides* a declaration of the same name in the scope that encloses the first scope. For example:

```
const double      NMPerSM = 0.826201;

double convertToSM(double nm)
{
    const double    NMPerSM = 0.826;

    return nm * NMPerSM;
}
```

Here, the local NMPerSM hides the declaration of NMPerSM with file scope. As a result, the value used in the computation is 0.826, not 0.826201.

In general, hiding names leads to errors that are difficult to discover. Therefore, this sort of thing should be avoided as much as possible.

Don't confuse hiding function names with overriding and overloading functions (see "Virtual Member Functions" and "Overloading Functions").

Declarations

A name must be declared within the necessary scope before it can be used. A declaration is often a definition as well. A name may be declared in multiple places throughout a program; however, it must be defined only once. If multiple declarations for a name exist, all must be identical.

The declaration of a function is a definition when you provide a body for the function; the declaration of a variable is a definition whenever storage is allocated. In short, a declaration is a definition except in the following situations:

- A variable is declared using the keyword `extern` (see "Storage Classes"), and no initializer is provided.
- The declaration is for a static data member; static data members are defined outside of their class.
- The declaration introduces a class name with no definition, in other words a forward declaration.
- The declaration is a prototype for a function; prototypes have no body.
- The declaration is a `typedef` statement, which declares a synonym for an existing type.

Declaring Variables

Declarations for variables introduce names that refer to data. They contain the following, in order: an optional storage class, optional qualifiers, a type, and a comma-delimited list of one or more names to declare. For example:

```
int             i, j, k;
char            buffer[80];
static int      counter, a;
volatile float  x;
```

Data members of classes are declared in a similar manner (see "Classes, Structs, and Unions"); however, they can only have the storage classes static (see "Static data members") and mutable (see "Mutable data members").

Declarations for variables may appear anywhere within a block, not just at the start. This makes code like the following common in C++:

```
void spin(int n)
{
    cout << "Spinning" << endl;

    for (int i = 0; i < n; i++)
        ;
}
```

In this example, the variable i is declared within the for loop, as opposed to at the start of the function in which the loop appears.

Pointer variables

Declarations for pointers follow the same rules as for other types of variables, except you must be sure to precede each name with an asterisk (*). For example:

```
int             *p, *q, *r;
```

Special situations arise when the qualifier const is used in the declaration of pointer variables (see "Qualifiers").

Initialization

Optionally, you can initialize variables using an initializer
where they are defined. Variables declared using the keyword const must be initialized. When an initializer appears,
it must evaluate to the correct type. For example:

```
bool            done = false;
static const int max = 100;
int             timers[] = {5, 5, 5};
int             *p, *q = 0, *r;
```

Arrays are initialized using initializer lists, as shown here for
the timers[] array, and in "Initializer lists for arrays." Variables that are instances of class types are initialized via constructors (see "Constructors"). Variables that are instances of
classes that do not explicitly define a constructor may be initialized using initializer lists similar in syntax to those used
for arrays. For example:

```
Rectangle       r = {0.0, 0.0, 3.0, 4.0};
```

If the class defines any constructor explicitly, this form of initialization cannot be used.

Declaring Functions

At their simplest, declarations for functions consist of the following: a return type, a name, and a comma-delimited list of
zero or more parameters enclosed by parentheses. Names are
not required for parameters, but they serve as good documentation. For example:

```
void            xchg(int &x, int &y);
```

Functions may be declared using the keyword static. Types
for parameters and return values may be qualified using
const and volatile. For example:

```
static char     *format(const char *s);
```

You can use references for parameters to have changes to the
parameters reflected in the caller's environment, as shown
for xchg (see "References").

Function definitions

Declarations for functions are called *prototypes*. They do not define a function; they simply inform the compiler of your intention to define and use it. To define a function, you specify a body for it, as follows:

```
void xchg(int &x, int &y)
{
   int t = x;
   x = y;
   y = t;
}
```

This function has a return type of void. If the return type is anything other than void, the function must use a return statement (see "Jump Statements") to return a value suitable for the function's return type. Functions that return void can use a return statement without a value.

Default arguments

Default arguments can be specified for the parameters of functions. You do this by setting a parameter equal to its default value in the function declaration, as shown below:

```
void               isTempOK(const int t,
                      const int low = 20,
                      const int high = 50);
```

A default argument is used for a parameter when nothing is specified for it in an invocation of the function. For example, assuming a temperature declared as temp, the following uses the default arguments 20 for low and 50 for high:

```
if (!isTempOK(temp))
{
   // Do something if too low or high.
}
```

If a function is declared with default arguments, the parameters with defaults must appear last in the parameter list. Values are assigned to parameters from left to right. Remaining parameters are then assigned their default values. Therefore, there is no way to provide an argument for a parameter after any that have assumed default values. So, for example, the following invocation passes 30 to low:

```
if (!isTempOK(temp, 30))
{
    // Do something if too low or high.
}
```

There is no way to pass 30 for high without also using an explicit argument for low.

Inline functions

An inline function is a function whose body is substituted directly at every point in a program where the function is called, as opposed to generating a call using the stack and a single copy of the function. To make a function inline, you precede its definition with the keyword inline, as follows:

```
inline void xchg(int &x, int &y)
{
    int t = x;
    x = y;
    y = t;
}
```

By inlining a function, you avoid the overhead required to set up each function call. However, since inlining requires that separate copies of the same function be inserted in potentially numerous places throughout your program, inlining is typically used only for very small functions. Because an inline function must be defined within every file in which it is used, inline functions are usually defined in header files.

NOTE

The inline keyword is just a request to the compiler to inline a function. The compiler makes the ultimate decision.

Storage Classes

The storage classes of C++ are static, extern, mutable, auto, and register. The storage class of a variable or data member determines its lifetime and linkage; the storage class of a function determines its linkage and other treatment. If no storage class is specified, the following rules apply:

Local variables
> Have the storage class auto by default.

Global variables
> Have file scope, unless declared using the keyword extern elsewhere.

Data members
> There is a separate instance of data members for each instance of their class.

Nonmember functions
> Have the storage class extern by default.

Member functions
> Must be invoked through an instance of their class.

static

The following list summarizes the meanings of the storage class static in various contexts:

Local variables
> Persist between executions of their enclosing block. They are constructed only once, or never if their declaration is never reached.

Global variables
> Have file scope. Unnamed namespaces are a better way to achieve this.

Data members
> A single instance of a static data member is shared by all instances of its class. Static data members are initialized before main is called.

Nonmember functions
> Have file scope. Unnamed namespaces offer a better way to achieve this.

Member functions
> Can be called without an instance of their class, but cannot themselves access members of their class that are not also declared static.

extern

When applied to a global variable or to a nonmember function, the extern storage class specifies that the variable or function is defined in another source file. Nonmember functions have the storage class extern by default.

mutable

The mutable storage class can be applied only to a class data member. It specifies that the member can be modified even though its containing object has been declared using the keyword const.

auto

The auto storage class instructs the compiler to allocate storage automatically for a variable on the stack each time a block is entered. Local variables are automatic by default; therefore, auto is rarely used.

register

The register storage class requests that the address of a variable be stored in a machine register for better performance. The register storage class is only a request; the compiler decides whether or not to use a register.

Qualifiers

The qualifiers of C++ are const and volatile. In some situations they are used together.

const

The const qualifier keeps the entity it qualifies from being modified, except for data members declared using keyword mutable (see "Storage Classes"). The following rules apply:

Local variables
> Once initialized, cannot be modified. They must be initialized.

Global variables
> Once initialized, cannot be modified. They must be initialized.

Data members
> Once initialized, cannot be modified. They must be initialized when an object is constructed.

Nonstatic member functions (where const appears at the end of the signature)
> Cannot modify nonstatic data members of their class except those declared using mutable. The member functions are allowed to be invoked through const instances of their class.

Function parameter
> Cannot be changed by the function.

Return value of a function
> Can be used only where a const value is permitted.

Pointer declarations use a syntax with const that depends on what you want to protect from modification. If you want to protect what a pointer addresses from being modified, you use a declaration like the following:

```
int          i = 100, j = 200;
const int    *p = &i;
```

```
*p = j;             // This is an error.
p = &j;             // This is OK.
```

This is the most common use. If you want to protect the
pointer itself from being modified, you use a declaration in
which const is written after the asterisk (*), as follows:

```
int                 i = 100, j = 200;
int *const          p = &i;

*p = j;             // This is OK.
p = &j;             // This is an error.
```

In the event that you want to protect both the data and the
pointer from being modified, you use a declaration that is a
combination of the two presented previously, as in this
example:

```
int                 i = 100, j = 200;
const int *const    p = &i;

p = &j;             // This is an error.
*p = j;             // This is an error.
```

volatile

The volatile qualifier informs the compiler that a variable,
data member, or parameter may be modified unexpectedly,
be it by another process, the hardware, or something else.
As a result, the compiler avoids optimizations that could
conflict with changes happening asynchronously to the
entity (e.g., normally a compiler will skip accessing memory
again if it needs a value that was just obtained in the previous
instruction).

When applied to member functions, volatile has a slightly
different shade of meaning. When you create a volatile object
of a class, the compiler will only allow you to call member
functions that have also been declared volatile. Thus, you
should apply the volatile qualifier to member functions in
cases when you expect to create volatile objects of a class,
and even then only apply volatile to those functions you
intend to invoke on those volatile objects.

Statements

There are many types of statements in C++. Some simply evaluate expressions, while others change the order in which statements are executed in the future.

Expression Statements

An *expression statement* is an expression followed by a single semicolon (;). Expression statements cause an expression to be evaluated. Side effects, such as an assignment to a variable, are completed before the next statement is executed. For example:

```
a = 10;
```

Null Statements

A *null statement* is written as a semicolon (;). Null statements are useful when the syntax of C++ requires a statement but you don't need anything performed. For example:

```
void spin(int n)
{
    for (int i = 0; i < n; i++)
        ;
}
```

This loop simply counts to a specified value, as might be required to insert a delay in a real-time system (assuming the compiler doesn't optimize the loop away altogether).

Compound Statements

A *compound statement* is a group of zero or more statements beginning with a left brace ({) and ending with a right brace (}). For example:

```
while (true)
{
    // Start of a compound statement.
    ...
```

```
    if (!done)
    {
        // Another compound statement.
    }
    else
    {
        // Another compound statement.
    }
}
```

Compound statements are often called *blocks*. A block defines a region that has its own local scope.

Iteration Statements

Iteration statements cause a statement or block to be executed repeatedly. There are three types of iteration statements in C++: while, do, and for.

while

A while loop repeats a statement or block as long as an expression (which can be a declaration) evaluated at the top of the loop is true. For example:

```
char            ch = 'y';

while (ch == 'y')
{
    // Do something to be repeated.
    ...

    cout << "Do it again (y or n)? ";
    cin  >> ch;
}
```

This repeats a block as long as ch is 'y'. The body of the loop is never executed if the expression at the top of the loop is false when the loop is first encountered.

do

A do loop repeats a statement or block as long as an expression evaluated at the bottom of the loop is true. For example:

```
char              ch;

do
{
   // Do something to be repeated.
   ...

   cout << "Do it again (y or n)? ";
   cin  >> ch;
} while (ch == 'y');
```

This repeats a block as long as ch is 'y'; however, the body of the loop is executed at least once because the condition for looping is evaluated at the end of each iteration.

for

A for loop is similar to a while loop, but additional mechanisms are provided for initializing the loop and making adjustments after each of its iterations. For example:

```
// Prevent warnings in Visual C++.
#pragma warning(disable:4786)

typedef map<int, string> IntStringMap;

IntStringMap     m;
char             s[4];

for (int i = 0; i < 10; i++)
{
   s[0] = 'a' + i; s[1] = 'b' + i;
   s[2] = 'c' + i; s[3] = '\0';

   m.insert(IntStringMap::value_type(i,
      string(s)));
}
```

The key to for loops is understanding the statements that go within the parentheses following the for keyword. The statement before the first semicolon is the statement executed to initialize the loop. Before each iteration, including the first, the expression between the two semicolons is evaluated. If the expression is true, the loop body is executed; otherwise, the loop terminates. After each iteration, the rightmost expression is evaluated, and the cycle is repeated. for loops can contain more complicated expressions as well. For example:

```
void upperString(char *t, const char *s)
{
    for (; *s != '\0'; *(t++) = toupper(*(s++)))
        ;

    *(t++) = '\0';
}
```

This function uses a for loop to translate string s to uppercase and copy it to t. The function assumes that storage has already been allocated for t. A null statement is used for initialization since s and t are already initialized when the function starts. A null statement is also used for the loop body.

NOTE

A name declared in a for initialization statement is visible until the end of the for loop.

Selection Statements

Selection statements execute a different statement or block based on the result produced by an expression. There are two types of selection statements in C++: if and switch.

if

An if statement evaluates an expression (which may be a declaration) and uses the result to determine which of up to two statements or blocks to execute next. For example:

```
if (i > 0 && i < 100)
{
    // Do something when within range.
}
else
{
    // Do something when not in range.
}
```

If the expression is true, the statement or block immediately after the terminating parentheses of the if section is executed; otherwise, the statement or block after else is executed. If the else clause is omitted, nothing is performed when the expression is not true. When if statements are nested within one another, else clauses associate with the nearest if.

switch

A switch statement selects one of several sections of code to execute based on the value of a controlling expression. For example:

```
switch (type)
{
    case keyDown:
        // Do something for a key down.
        ...
        break;

    case keyUp:
        // Do something for a key up.
        ...
        break;
    ...
    default:
        // Handle anything not handled.
        ...
}
```

Each section is identified by the keyword case followed by an expression that must evaluate to a distinct, constant, integral value at compile time. At runtime, execution branches to the section identified by the value matching that of the controlling expression, and continues from that point onward. A break statement (see "Jump Statements") is used at the end of each case to prevent the code associated with all subsequent cases from being executed. An optional default case can be provided to handle the situation when the value of the controlling expression does not match any of the cases.

Jump Statements

Jump statements jump unconditionally to a different statement. There are four types of jump statements in C++: break, continue, goto, and return.

break

A break statement is used to jump out of an innermost loop or switch statement. For example:

```
for (;;)
{
   if (done)
      break;

   // When we're done, set done to true
   // so we break on the next iteration.
   ...
}
```

This is a for loop that has no condition specified for stopping it. A break statement is used to break out of the loop when done is true.

continue

A continue statement is used to jump to the start of an innermost enclosing loop. For example:

```
while (!done)
{
   // If we need to skip the end portion
   // of the function, set skip to true.
   ...

   if (skip)
      continue;

   // This gets skipped when continuing.
   ...
}
```

This is a while loop that contains statements to be skipped when skip has been set to true. A continue statement is used to jump to the start of the loop in order to skip these statements.

goto

A goto statement jumps to a label that you specify. For example:

```
if (GetLastError( ) != ERROR_SUCCESS)
   goto handleError;

// This code gets skipped on an error.
...

handleError:
// Do something to handle error state.
```

Because goto statements lead to unstructured code, they are seldom used.

return

A return statement jumps out of a function, and if needed sets a return value. For example:

```
double convertToSM(double nm)
{
   return nm * NMPerSM;
}
```

A return statement can be called from anywhere within a function. The type of the value returned must be, or be convertible to, the return type of the function. Functions that return void do not require return statements. For example:

```
void sayHello( )
{
   cout << "Hello" << endl;
}
```

A return is performed automatically when this function completes. However, a return statement with no value can be used to jump out of the function before the end of the function block is reached.

Namespaces

A namespace defines a named scope. Namespaces are used to group related names and to avoid clashes between similar names in different parts of large programs. You declare a namespace as follows:

```
namespace Aviation
{
    const double    NMPerSM = 0.826201;

    double          convertToSM(double nm);
}
```

Namespaces can contain anything that you would otherwise declare outside of a namespace, even other namespaces. In addition, namespaces are open, which means you can extend a namespace using multiple declarations. For example, the following extends the previous declaration of Aviation:

```
namespace Aviation
{
    const double    SMPerNM = 1.21036;

    double          convertToNM(double sm);
}
```

You use a name outside of its declaring namespace by qualifying it with the name of the namespace using the scope operator (::). For example:

```
Aviation::convertToSM(20.0);
```

To define this function outside of the namespace, you do the following:

```
double Aviation::convertToSM(double nm)
{
    return nm * NMPerSM;
}
```

Names not declared within a namespace belong to a special namespace: the *global namespace*. To avoid qualifying names everywhere they are used, you use a using declaration or directive.

using Declarations

A using declaration lets you use a name from a namespace without having to qualify it. For example:

```cpp
namespace Aviation
{
    double      convertToSM(double nm);
    double      convertToNM(double sm);
}
...
using Aviation::convertToSM;
...
double          sm = convertToSM(20.0);
```

A using declaration adds a name to the scope in which the using declaration exists. This means the following:

- A compilation error occurs if the name is declared elsewhere in the same scope.
- If the same name is declared in an enclosing scope, the name in the namespace hides it.

using Directives

A using directive lets you use all names from a namespace without qualifying them. For example:

```cpp
namespace Aviation
{
    double      convertToSM(double nm);
    double      convertToNM(double sm);
}
...
using namespace Aviation;
...
```

```
double          sm = convertToSM(20.0);
double          nm = convertToNM(40.0);
```

A using directive does not add a name to the current scope; it only makes a name accessible from it. This means the following:

- If a name is declared elsewhere within a local scope, the name in the namespace is hidden once the local declaration occurs.

- A name in the namespace hides the same name declared in an enclosing scope.

- A compilation error occurs when the same name is made visible from multiple namespaces, or if a name in the namespace hides a name in the global namespace.

Unnamed Namespaces

A namespace is unnamed when you omit the name for it in its declaration. For example:

```
namespace
{
...
}
```

The names in an unnamed namespace have file scope. Considering this, they are like variables or functions declared as static without declaring each explicitly using the static keyword. Since there is no way to refer to an unnamed namespace, a using directive is implied after the namespace declaration. Unnamed namespaces are the preferred means of declaring variables and functions with file scope.

Classes, Structs, and Unions

Classes are types that group data and functionality together into encapsulated, cohesive units. Structs and unions are similar to classes, but differ in the ways outlined later under

---

"Structs" and "Unions." Classes, structs, and unions are collectively called *class types*. You define a class by declaring a set of data members and member functions for it. For example:

```
class Account
{
public:
                Account(double b);

    void        deposit(double amt);
    void        withdraw(double amt);
    double      getBalance() const;

private:
    double      balance;
};
```

This class declares one data member (balance) and three member functions (deposit, withdraw, and getBalance). One constructor is declared to perform initialization. The keywords public and private control how various parts of the class can be accessed (see "Access Levels for Members").

Declaring Objects

Objects are specific instances of a class. The following declares an object that is an instance of Account:

```
Account         account(100.0);
```

This declaration is also a definition because storage is allocated for the object. The rules for declaring and defining objects essentially follow the rules presented under "Declaring Variables," except when it comes to initialization (see "Constructors").

Accessing Members

To access a member of an object, you use the dot form of the selection operator (.). For example, the following assigns 500 to the data member i of an object called object:

```
object.i = 500;
```

The following invokes the member function f of object, passing it two arguments, a and b:

```
object.f(a, b);
```

To access a member of an object using a pointer to the object, you use the arrow form of selection (->). For example, the following assigns 500 to the data member i of an object referenced by objptr:

```
objptr->i = 500;
```

The following invokes the member function f of the object referenced by objptr passing it two arguments, a and b:

```
objptr->f(a, b);
```

To access a member from within the class in which it is defined, or from within a derived class (see "Inheritance"), usually you specify only the name of the member, unless accessing the member through the this pointer. By whatever means you access a member, the compiler either allows or denies access based on the member's access level (see "Access Levels for Members").

Declaring Data Members

You declare the data members for a class in the class's definition. For example:

```
class Account
{
...
private:
    double      balance;
};
```

The rules for declaring and defining data members in a class are similar to those for variables (see "Declaring Variables"), with the following exceptions:

- You cannot use an initializer with a nonstatic data member where the member is defined. (Static members are defined outside of the class.)

- The only storage classes allowed for data members are static and mutable (see "Storage Classes").

Each instantiation of a class gets its own copy of data members, except those declared using the keyword static. The declaration of a nonstatic data member also defines the data member.

Static data members

Static data members are shared by all instances of a class. You declare a static data member using the keyword static. For example:

```
class Account
{
public:
...
    void            deposit(double amt)
                    {
                        ...
                        deposits++;
                    }
...
private:
...
    static int      deposits;
};
```

Unlike the declaration of a nonstatic data member, the declaration of a static data member does not define it. You must define a static data member outside of the class, at which point you usually initialize it as well. For example:

```
int                 Account::deposits = 0;
```

You qualify a static data member outside of its class with the name of the class using the scope operator (::). You can refer to a static data member without an instantiation of the class. The access level for a static data member does not apply when defining the member (see "Access Levels for Members").

Constant data members

Constant data members cannot be modified at any point in an object's lifetime. You declare a constant data member with the keyword const. For example:

```
class Account
{
...
private:
...
    const double       minBalance;
};
```

Because constant data members cannot be modified, they must be initialized using an initializer in the constructor for the class (see "Member initializers"). However, data members declared using both the keywords const and static (see below) are initialized as described under "Static data members."

```
class Account
{
...
private:
...
    static const double minBalance;
};
```

You declare a constant data member as static when its value is to be the same for all instances of the class. This saves memory because all instances of the class share the same member.

Mutable data members

Mutable data members are modifiable even when the object that contains them has been declared using the keyword const. You declare a mutable data member using the keyword mutable. For example:

```
class Account
{
public:
                Account(double b)
                {
                   balance = b;
                }

    double      getBalance() const
                {
                   counter++;
                   return balance;
                }
...
private:
    mutable int counter;
    double      balance;
};
```

In the following example, even though a is declared using const, its mutable data member counter can be modified (via getBalance) to count the number of times the balance is accessed for the object:

```
const Account   a(100.0);

a.getBalance();   // Increments counter.
```

Volatile data members

The volatile qualifier informs the compiler that the data member may be modified unexpectedly, be it by another process, the hardware, or something else. You declare a volatile data member by preceding it with volatile (similar to const).

Declaring Member Functions

Member functions are functions declared as members of a class. You declare the member functions for a class in the class's definition. For example:

```
class Account
{
public:
...
   void           deposit(double amt);
   void           withdraw(double amt);
   double         getBalance() const;
...
};
```

The rules for declaring and defining member functions are similar to those for functions that are not class members (see "Declaring Functions"), with the following exceptions:

- You can declare member functions using the keyword virtual to support polymorphism (see "Virtual Member Functions").
- The only storage class allowed for member functions is static.

When you declare a member function, you can either define it or wait to provide a definition outside of the class. To define a member function where it is declared, you follow the signature of the function with its body. For example:

```
class Account
{
public:
...
   void           deposit(double amt)
                  {
                      balance += amt;
                  }
...
private:
   double         balance;
};
```

Member functions defined within a class definition are treated as inline (see "Inline functions") unless they are also declared using the keyword `virtual` (see "Virtual Member Functions"). In a definition outside of the class, you qualify the member function with the name of its class using the scope operator (`::`). For example:

```
void Account::deposit(double amt)
{
    balance += amt;
}
```

You can also request that a member function defined outside of its class be treated as inline by preceding the definition with the keyword `inline`.

NOTE

Definitions of member functions outside of their class belong in the source file for the class, not in the class's header file (see "Header Files"). Otherwise, the member function ends up being defined more than once when the header file is included multiple times. The exceptions to this are definitions of member functions preceded by the keyword `inline`, and those implementing template classes; these go in header files.

The this pointer

All member functions not declared using the keyword `static` (see "Static member functions") have a special pointer, called `this`, that points to the instantiating object. When you access members within the class where they are defined, the `this` pointer is implied, so usually you omit it. For example:

```
class Account
{
public:
...
    void            deposit(double amt)
                    {
                        balance += amt;
```

```
                         }
    ...
    private:
       double        balance;
    };
```

implies:

```
    class Account
    {
    public:
    ...
       void          deposit(double amt)
                     {
                         this->balance += amt;
                     }
    ...
    private:
       double        balance;
    };
```

Sometimes you need to specify the this pointer explicitly, as
in the following example of overloading the assignment operator for the Account class:

```
    Account &Account::operator=(const Account
       &a)
    {
       // Don't assign an account to itself.
       if (this != &a)
       {
           // Copy each member, as necessary.
       }

       // Returning a reference to an Account
       // makes chained assignments possible.
       return *this;
    }
```

Static member functions

Static member functions can be invoked with or without an
instance of the class. You declare a static member function
using the keyword static. For example:

```
    class Account
    {
```

```
public:
...
    static int    getDeposits( )
                  {
                      return deposits;
                  }
...
private:
...
    static int    deposits;
};
```

To invoke a static member function from outside of its class without using an object, you qualify it with the name of the class using the scope operator (::). For example:

```
int total = Account::getDeposits( );
```

Because static member functions do not have to be invoked through an instance of the class, they do not have a this pointer. As a result, they can only directly access data members or member functions of the class that are static themselves.

Constant member functions

Constant member functions are the only nonstatic member functions that can be invoked from objects declared using the keyword const. You declare a constant member function by appending const to its signature. For example:

```
class Account
{
public:
...
    double        getBalance( ) const;
...
};
```

A const member function is not allowed to modify nonstatic data members of the class except those declared using the keyword mutable, or to call member functions not declared using const themselves.

Volatile member functions

Volatile member functions are the only nonstatic member functions that can be invoked from objects declared using the keyword volatile. You declare a volatile member function by appending volatile to its signature (similar to const). See "volatile" under "Qualifiers" for more information.

Access Levels for Members

The access level of a member determines from where in a program you are allowed to use it. You assign an access level to a member using one of three access specifiers:

public
> Public members can be accessed anywhere, including outside of the class itself.

protected
> Protected members can be accessed within the class in which they are declared and within derived classes.

private
> Private members can be accessed only within the class in which they are declared.

Access specifiers are always followed by a colon (:). For example:

```
class Account
{
public:
                Account(double b);

    void        deposit(double amt);
    void        withdraw(double amt);
    void        getBalance() const;

private:
    double      balance;
};
```

Access specifiers are applied according to the following rules:

- If no access specifier is specified at the start of a class, the members in that portion of the class are private by default.
- The default access level for structs and unions is public.
- The access level of a member is defined by the most recent access specifier appearing before it in the class definition.
- An access specifier can be used any number of times within a class definition.
- The access level of a member does not apply when defining the member outside of its class (see "Static data members").

Friends

Friends of classes are granted access to all members of the class. You can declare functions (including member functions of other classes) or entire classes as friends of a class. For example:

```
class Account
{
    friend class    AccountManager;

    friend void     doDefaultDebit(Account
                        &a);

    friend void     ATM::deductFee(Account
                        &a, double fee);

public:
                    Account(double b);

    void            deposit(double amt);
    void            withdraw(double amt);
    void            getBalance() const;

private:
    double          balance;
};
```

The following rules apply to friends:

- Declarations of friends can appear anywhere within a class definition, but usually appear at the beginning.

- The access specifier under which friends appear makes no difference.

- Friendship is not inherited, nor do friends of nested classes have any special access rights to the members of their enclosing class.

- Functions first declared as friends have external linkage; otherwise, they retain their linkage.

Constructors

Constructors are special member functions used to initialize instances of a class. They give you the opportunity to perform initialization (e.g., allocating dynamic storage for data members, opening files, etc.) before an object is ever used. Constructors are called whenever storage is allocated for an object, whether automatically by the compiler or when you use new or new[] (see "Memory Management"). See "Constructors and Inheritance" for information about constructors and base classes.

Constructors have the same name as the class and never return a value. For example:

```
class Account
{
public:
                    Account(double b);
...
};
```

You can provide the definition for a constructor either where you declare the constructor or outside of the class, as shown below:

```
Account::Account(double b)
{
    balance = b;
}
```

Often constructors are overloaded, so there is more than one way to initialize instances of a class. When allocating an array of objects using new[ ], there must be a default constructor available, either provided by you or synthesized by the compiler.

Default constructors

Default constructors are constructors that take no arguments or that have default values specified for all arguments. To instantiate an object using its default constructor, use one of the following approaches:

```
Account         account;
Account         *p = new Account;
```

If you do not define any constructors for a class, the compiler synthesizes a default constructor for you. The default constructor supplied by the compiler calls the default constructor for each member of the class.

Copy constructors

Copy constructors are special constructors that accept a reference to an instance of their own class (usually a const instance). For example:

```
class Account
{
public:
            Account(const Account &a);
...
};
```

Copy constructors copy the instance of the class supplied as an argument into the instantiating object. They can accept additional arguments, provided default values are specified for them (see "Default arguments"). Copy constructors are invoked by the compiler in the following situations:

- An instance of a class is passed by value to a function.
- An instance of a class is returned from a function.

- An instance of a class is initialized to another instance using an initializer.
- An instance of a class is provided explicitly as a single argument to the constructor.

If you do not provide a copy constructor for a class, the compiler synthesizes one that does a member-by-member copy. When you define a copy constructor for a class, often you also overload the assignment operator (see "Overloading Operators").

Explicit constructors

Constructors declared as explicit do not take part in implicit conversions (see "Type Conversions"). You use the keyword explicit to declare a constructor as explicit. For example:

```
class Account
{
public:
    explicit        Account(double b)
                    {
                        balance = b;
                    }
    ...
private:
    double          balance;
};
```

Because this constructor is declared as explicit, the compiler disallows the following, which requires an implicit conversion from double to Account:

```
Account             account = 100.0;
```

You declare only constructors that take one argument as explicit, since these are the only constructors used in implicit conversions.

Member initializers

Member initializers stipulate how to initialize data members even before the constructor is executed. Member initializers are specified with a constructor's definition. They are placed in a comma-delimited list between the constructor's signature and its body. The list begins with a colon (:). For example:

```
class Account
{
public:
                Account(double b) :
                    balance(b),
                    minBalance(25.0)
                {
                }
    ...
private:
    double      balance;
    const double    minBalance;
};
```

The following rules apply:

- Nonstatic data members declared as const or references must be initialized using a member initializer because they cannot be modified at any point in the object's lifetime.

- You initialize data members that are objects by providing a comma-delimited list of arguments within the parentheses of the member initializer. The arguments must be suited to a constructor of the object.

- Initialization is performed in the order in which the data members are declared in the class, not the order in which members appear in the initializer list.

- Static data members cannot be initialized using member initializers; you initialize them where they are defined outside of the class.

Destructors

Destructors are special member functions invoked when an instance of a class is about to be destroyed. They give you the opportunity to clean up (e.g., reclaim dynamic storage used by data members, close files, etc.) before an object goes away. Destructors are called just before an object goes out of scope and when you destroy objects explicitly via a pointer to them using delete or delete[] (see "Memory Management"). See "Destructors and Inheritance" for information about destructors and base classes, including the importance of virtual destructors.

Destructors have the same name as their class, but preceded by a tilde (~). They take no arguments and return no value. The following example declares a constructor named ~Account:

```
class Account
{
public:
                ~Account();
...
};
```

You can provide the definition for a destructor either where you declare the destructor or outside of the class, as shown below:

```
Account::~Account()
{
...
}
```

On rare occasions, you may have a reason to call a destructor explicitly. The following invokes the destructor of Account via an Account pointer p:

```
p->~Account();
```

So that you don't have to be concerned about whether a destructor exists for a class, C++ allows such a call regardless of whether or not a destructor has been defined. If no destructor is defined for the class or a base class, the call has no effect. This mechanism does not enable you to call a destructor that is defined but that has an access level making it unreachable (e.g., private).

Nested Declarations

Anything declared inside of a class has class scope (see "Scope"). In addition to data members and member functions, a class definition may contain declarations for enumerations, namespaces, and even other classes, as well as type definitions using typedef. For example:

```
class Account
{
public:
    enum Status
    {
                Premier,
                Valued,
                Standard
    };

    enum
    {
                LargePIN = 8,
                SmallPIN = 4
    };
    ...
    void        setStatus(Status s);
    void        setMinPIN(int n);
...
};
```

Outside of the class, you qualify a name declared within the class using the class name with the scope operator (::), as follows:

```
Account         *p = new Account;

p->setMinPIN(Account::LargePIN);
p->setStatus(Account::Status::Valued);
```

Whenever you use a name declared within a class, the compiler either grants or denies you access based on the access level under which the name was declared (see "Access Levels for Members").

Forward Declarations

You can declare a class without providing a definition for it. You do that using what is called a *forward declaration*, which declares the class name without specifying any other details about the class. For example:

```
class Account;
```

This informs the compiler that you plan to define the class later but are going to use its name now without referring to any of the class's members. For example, forward declarations are needed when two classes refer to each other:

```
class Account;

class Bank
{
...
private:
   Account       *accounts;
};

class Account
{
...
private:
   Bank          *bank;
};
```

Alternatively, you could define Account first and provide a forward declaration for Bank.

Structs

Structs are functionally identical to classes except that the default access level for their members is public, not private. To define a struct, you use the keyword struct in place of the keyword class.

Unions

Unions are similar to classes; however, they can hold a value for only one data member at a time. As a result, a union occupies only as much space as its largest data member requires. Other differences between unions and classes are:

- The default access level for unions is public; the default access level for classes is private.
- Unions cannot have member functions that are declared using the keyword virtual.
- Unions cannot inherit from anything, nor can anything inherit from them.
- The members of unions cannot be objects that define constructors or destructors, or that overload the assignment operator.

Unions can be anonymous (unnamed). This form is used when nesting a union inside of a struct or class that contains an extra data member to indicate what the union contains. For example:

```
struct AccountInfo
{
    enum
    {
                NameInfo,
                BalanceInfo
    };

    int         type;

    union
    {
        char    name[20];
        double  balance;
    };
};
```

When setting a value in the union, you record how the union is being used. For example:

```
AccountInfo      info;

info.type = AccountInfo::BalanceInfo;
info.balance = 100.0;
```

Whenever you need to access the data member, you check what the union contains. For example:

```
if (info.type == AccountInfo::BalanceInfo)
{
    // Use the balance.
}
```

Inheritance

When you derive one class from another, the derived class inherits the data members and member functions that the other class defines (subject to access controls) while adding its own. Aside from the benefits that inheritance offers stemming from the reuse of functionality provided by the base class, inheritance is fundamental to supporting polymorphism (see "Virtual Member Functions"), an essential part of object-oriented programming. Consider the version of Account below:

```
class Account
{
public:
                Account(double b);

    void        deposit(double amt);
    void        withdraw(double amt);
    double      getBalance() const;

protected:
    double      balance;
};
```

To derive a new class called BankAccount from Account, you do the following:

```
class BankAccount : public Account
{
public:
                BankAccount(double r);

    void        addInterest();
    void        chargeFee(double c);
```

```
private:
    double          interestRate;
};
```

Account is called the *base class* (or *superclass*). BankAccount is called the *derived class* (or *subclass*). A BankAccount object gives you the functionality of both BankAccount and Account:

```
BankAccount         bankAccount(2.25);

bankAccount.deposit(50.0);
bankAccount.addInterest( );
```

Access to members of the base class depends on two criteria: the access level of the member in the base class (see "Access Levels for Members") and the access level for inheritance (see "Access Levels for Inheritance").

Constructors and Inheritance

Whenever you instantiate an object of a class derived from another class, multiple constructors are called so that each class in the derivation chain can initialize itself (see "Constructors").

Order of construction

The constructor for each class in the derivation chain is called beginning with the base class at the top of the derivation chain and ending with the most derived class.

Base class initializers

Base class initializers stipulate the data to pass to the constructors of base classes. They are specified with a constructor's definition. Base class initializers are placed in a comma-delimited list between the constructor's signature and its body. The list begins with a colon (:). For example:

```
class BankAccount : public Account
{
public:
                    BankAccount(double r) :
```

```
                    Account(0.0),
                    interestRate(r)
                {
                }
    ...
    private:
        double          interestRate;
    };
```

This class also contains a member initializer for `interestRate`. Here's some other information you need to know about using base class initializers:

- If a base class does not have a default constructor, the derived class must provide a base class initializer for it.
- Base class initializers frequently appear alongside member initializers, which use a similar syntax.
- If more than one argument is required by a base class constructor, the arguments are separated by commas.

Destructors and Inheritance

Whenever an object of a class derived from another class is about to be destroyed, the destructor for each class in the derivation chain, if defined, is called (see "Destructors").

Order of destruction

The destructor for each class in the derivation chain is called beginning with the most derived class and ending with the base class at the top of the derivation chain.

Virtual destructors

When deleting an object using a base class pointer or reference, it is essential that destructors for each of the classes in the derivation chain get the chance to run:

```
    BankAccount         *bptr;
    Account             *aptr;

    bptr = new BankAccount(2.25);
```

```
aptr = bptr;
...
delete aptr;
```

To ensure that the destructors of all classes in the derivation chain are called, the destructor in the base class must be declared using the keyword `virtual` (see "Virtual Member Functions"). For example:

```
class Account
{
public:
    virtual        ~Account( )
                   {
                       ...
                   }
...
};
```

NOTE

Not declaring a destructor using the keyword `virtual` in a class from which other classes are later derived is a common source of memory leaks and other unexpected behavior. This is because only the destructor of the pointer's class is called; no polymorphic behavior occurs.

Virtual Member Functions

To give a member function from a base class new behavior in a derived class, you *override* it. This must not be confused with the process by which you *overload* a member function (see "Overloading Functions").

To allow a member function in a base class to be overridden, you declare the member function using the keyword `virtual` in the base class. For example:

```
class Account
{
public:
...
    virtual void   withdraw(double amt)
```

```
                        {
                            balance -= amt;
                        }

protected:
    double          balance;
};
```

The member function in the derived class is declared like any
other member function, although it is common to declare the
member function using the keyword virtual in the derived
class as well for purposes of documentation. For example:

```
class BankAccount : public Account
{
public:
...
    virtual void    withdraw(double amt)
                    {
                        if (balance - amt < 0.0)
                        {
                            // Do nothing.
                        }
                        else
                        {
                            // Balance OK.
                            balance -= amt;
                        }
                    }
...
};
```

When you invoke a virtual member function via a base class
pointer or reference to an object of a derived class, the member function of the derived class is called instead of the member function of the base class. For example:

```
BankAccount         bankAccount(2.25);
Account             *aptr = &bankAccount;

aptr->withdraw(50.0);
```

The last line in this example calls withdraw of the BankAccount
class. To determine which member function to call, C++
uses *polymorphism*, or *dynamic binding*. This allows the

determination to be made based on the actual type of the object addressed by the base class pointer or reference at runtime.

The following rules apply to virtual member functions:

- Constructors cannot be virtual, but destructors can be. In fact, there are good reasons to almost always make destructors virtual (see "Virtual destructors").

- Declaring a member function using the keyword `virtual` in a base class does not require that you override it in the derived class unless the member function is declared pure virtual (see "Abstract Base Classes") in the base class and you plan to instantiate the derived class.

- Once a member function has been declared using the keyword `virtual` in a base class, it is virtual from that point on in the derivation chain.

- The parameter list and return type for the member function in the derived class must match those of the member function in the base class. Otherwise, the member function of the derived class hides the member function in the base class, and no polymorphic behavior will occur.

- If you don't declare a member function using the keyword `virtual` in the base class, the same member function in the derived class hides the member function in the base class (see "Enclosing Scopes"), and no polymorphic behavior will occur.

- A virtual member function that is private in the base class can be overridden in a derived class even though it cannot be accessed via the derived class. A call to the member function from within the base class uses polymorphism to invoke the member function of the appropriate derived class.

The decision of whether to allow a member function to be called based on its access level is made at compile time. Since the decision of which member function to call using polymorphism is made at runtime, it is possible that a member function of a derived class with a less restrictive access level in the base class could be invoked from a point that seemingly defies its access level.

Abstract Base Classes

An *abstract base class*, not to be confused with a virtual base class, is a class that contains one or more *pure virtual* member functions. You make a member function pure virtual using the keyword virtual and appending the pure specifier, = 0, to the signature of the member function in the class definition. For example:

```
class Account
{
public:
...
    virtual double estimateReturn( ) = 0;
...
};
```

The following rules apply:

- A class containing one or more pure virtual member functions cannot be instantiated.

- An abstract base class prescribes an interface to be implemented by a derived class. A derived class may provide a definition for a member function of the base class, declare them as pure virtual itself, or not declare it at all. In the latter two cases, the derived class becomes abstract as well.

- A pure virtual member function can be defined in the class that declares it pure virtual.

- If you declare the destructor of a class pure virtual, you must provide a definition for it in the class in which you declare it pure virtual.

Access Levels for Inheritance

Access levels for inheritance influence the extent to which members inherited from base classes are accessible in derived classes. You assign an access level for inheritance using one

---

of three access specifiers `public`, `protected`, or `private` before the name of the base class. For example:

```
class BankAccount : public Account
{
...
};
```

In this context, the access specifiers have the following meanings:

public
> Public members in the base class remain public in the derived class. Protected members in the base class remain protected in the derived class. Public inheritance yields an "is a" relationship between the derived class and the base class.

protected
> Public and protected members in the base class are protected in the derived class. Protected inheritance yields an "implemented in terms of" relationship between the derived class and the base class.

private
> Public and protected members in the base class become private in the derived class. Private inheritance yields a stricter "implemented in terms of" relationship between the derived class and the base class.

Multiple Inheritance

To derive a class from several base classes at once, you specify the name of each class in a comma-delimited list that begins with a colon (:) after the name of the derived class. You precede each class in the list with an access level for inheritance (see "Access Levels for Inheritance"). For example, the `CheckingAccount` class below uses multiple inheritance:

```
class Account
{
public:
```

```
...
   double          getBalance( ) const
                   {
                       return balance;
                   }
...
protected:
   double          balance;
};

class BankAccount : public Account
{
...
};

class WireAccount : public Account
{
...
};

class CheckingAccount : public
   BankAccount, public WireAccount
{
...
};
```

With multiple inheritance, when any of the base classes from which the class is derived have a base class in common themselves, multiple instances of that common base class occur in objects instantiated from the derived class. For example, CheckingAccount objects get two balance data members and two getBalance methods. As a result, this invocation of getBalance is ambiguous and results in a compilation error:

```
CheckingAccount    c(100.0);

// This results in a compilation error.
double b0 = c.getBalance( );
```

Instead, you must qualify the method with the specific instance of the base class that you desire by explicitly specifying a path to it in the derivation hierarchy, as follows:

```
double b1 = c.BankAccount::getBalance( );
double b2 = c.WireAccount::getBalance( );
```

If this duplication of base class members is not what you desire, you can make use of a virtual base class.

Virtual Base Classes

A *virtual base class*, not to be confused with an abstract base class, remedies the situation in multiple inheritance whereby multiple instances of a base class are included in objects of a derived class. To make a base class virtual, you include the keyword `virtual` where the class is specified as a base class. For example, the following makes `Account` a virtual base class:

```
class Account
{
public:
...
    double          getBalance() const
                    {
                        return balance;
                    }
...
protected:
    double          balance;
};

class BankAccount : virtual public
    Account
{
...
};

class WireAccount : virtual public
    Account
{
...
};

class CheckingAccount : public
    BankAccount, public WireAccount
{
...
};
```

Instances of CheckingAccount get a single balance data member and a single getBalance method. As a result, the invocation of getBalance presented under "Multiple Inheritance" is no longer ambiguous.

Templates

Templates are blueprints from which versions of a class or function are generated automatically by the compiler based on a set of parameters. Each time you use a template with a different set of parameters, a new version of the class or function is generated to suit how you are trying to use it. Each new version of the class or function is called a *specialization* of the template.

Template Classes

To parameterize a template class, you precede its definition with the keyword template. Template parameters, which can be type or nontype parameters, are placed in a comma-delimited list enclosed by angle brackets. Type parameters are preceded by the keyword class or typename. You use type parameters in place of specific types within the class definition. For example:

```
template <class Type>
class Array
{
public:
...
    bool            insert(const Type
                        &element, int pos);
...
private:
    Type            *bufferForElements;
};
```

This template class uses a single type parameter called Type. The template serves as a blueprint for arrays that contain elements of any one type. See "Nontype parameters in template classes" for information on nontype parameters.

Instantiation of template classes

To instantiate a template class, you specify arguments for the
template along with the name of the class itself wherever the
class is used. You specify arguments for a template class as a
comma-delimited list enclosed by angle brackets after the
class name. For example, the following creates an array of
integers and an array of Account objects:

```
Array<int>        counters;
Array<Account>    accounts;
```

Types used as arguments cannot be classes with local scope.
Once a template class has been instantiated, you use it like
any other class.

Member functions in template classes

Member functions defined outside of the template class in
which they are declared must be parameterized as well. For
example:

```
template <class Type>
bool Array<Type>::insert(const Type
    &element, int pos)
{
...
}
```

This defines the insert member function for the template
class Array. You can define a constructor for the class as
follows:

```
template <class Type>
Array<Type>::Array<Type>()
{
```

```
   ...
}
```

Explicit specialization of template classes

An *explicit specialization* of a template class defines a specific form of the template to use for a certain set of parameters. To define an explicit specialization, you use the keyword `template` with an empty pair of angle brackets. After the class name, you specify a comma-delimited list of parameters, in angle brackets, to which the specialization applies. For example:

```
template<>
class Array<void *>
{
public:
                Array(int elmtSize);

    bool        insert(const void *
                    element, int pos);
...
private:
    void        *bufferForElements;
};
```

This specialization stipulates that an instantiation of the `Array` template class with a `void` pointer should use this form of the template as opposed to any other. For example:

```
Array<void *>    counters(sizeof(int));
```

You can define any number of explicit specializations to override the primary template for a class.

Nontype parameters in template classes

Nontype parameters in template classes are constant values that you can use in the class definition. Nontype parameters consist of a type followed by a name. For example, the following template class has s as a nontype parameter:

```
template <class Type, int s>
class Array
{
```

```
public:
...
    bool            insert(const Type
                        &element, int pos);
...
private:
    Type            elements[s];
};
```

You specify a value for a nontype parameter where the template class is instantiated, as shown below:

```
Array<float, 50> temperatureValues;
```

This instantiates an array containing 50 elements of type float. Nontype parameters must be one of the following types: an integral type, enumeration, pointer, reference, or pointer to member. Arguments specified for them must be constant. Pointers and references must address objects or functions with external linkage (see "Storage Classes").

Default arguments for template classes

Template classes, unlike templates for functions, can be defined with default arguments, except with explicit specialization. You set a type parameter equal to its default type, or a nontype parameter equal to its default value, where the template class is defined. If you omit the argument when you instantiate the template, the default is used.

Template Functions

To parameterize a template function, you precede its definition with the keyword template. Template parameters, which can be type or nontype parameters, are placed in a comma-delimited list enclosed by angle brackets. Type parameters are preceded by the keyword class or typename. You use type parameters in place of specific types within the function definition. For example:

```
template <class Type>
void xchg(Type &x, Type &y)
{
```

```
    Type t = x;
    x = y;
    y = t;
};
```

This template function uses a single type parameter called Type. The template serves as a blueprint for any function that swaps two values of like type. See "Nontype parameters in template functions" for information on nontype parameters.

Instantiation of template functions

The compiler generates an appropriate instance of a template function based on the arguments you use when calling it. You call a template function just as you do any other. For example:

```
int             i = 10, j = 20;
Account         a(50.0), b(75.0);

xchg(i, j);
xchg(a, b);
```

Arguments to template functions

Template functions often take template classes as arguments, as do member functions of template classes. For example, assuming Array is defined as shown under "Template Classes," you can do the following:

```
template <class Type>
bool insert(Array<Type> &a, const Type
    &element, int pos)
{
    return a.insert(element, pos);
}
```

Explicit specialization of template functions

An explicit specialization of a template function defines a specific form of the template to use for a certain set of parameters. To define an explicit specialization, you use the keyword template with an empty pair of angle brackets. After the function name, you specify a comma-delimited list of parameters, in angle brackets, to which the specialization applies. For example:

```
template<>
void xchg<string>(string &s, string &t)
{
    s.swap(t);
};
```

This specialization stipulates that the invocation of the xchg template function, like that shown below, should use this form of the template as opposed to any other:

```
string          s1("abc"), s2("xyz");

xchg<string>(s1, s2);
```

You can define any number of explicit specializations to override the primary template for a function.

Nontype parameters in template functions

Nontype parameters in template functions are constant values that you can use in the function definition. Nontype parameters consist of a type followed by a name. For example, the following template function has n as a nontype parameter:

```
template <class Type, int n>
void sort(Array<Type> &a)
{
    // Only sort up to position n.
}
```

To specify a nontype parameter where a template function that has a nontype parameter is invoked, do the following:

```
Array<int>          integerArray;
...
// Sort only the first 10 values.
sort<int, 10>(integerArray);
```

Arguments specified for nontype parameters must be constant. See "Nontype parameters in template classes" for the types of values that are allowed for nontype parameters.

Overloading

Overloading allows you to provide more than one definition for a function within the same scope. It also lets you define additional behaviors for most operators.

Overloading Functions

To overload a function, you give it several definitions, each uniquely identifiable by the arguments it accepts; return type is not considered. The compiler decides the definition to use based on the arguments provided when the function is called. For example:

```
char *min(char *s, char *t)
{
    return (strcmp(s, t) < 0) ? s : t;
}

float min(float x, float y)
{
    return (x < y) ? x : y;
}
```

The first definition is used when min is called with two character pointers. The second is used when min is called with two floating-point values. For example, you could call min in either of the ways below:

```
char       *s = min("abc", "xyz");
float      f  = min(4.56F, 1.23F);
```

To choose the definition to use, the compiler first searches for a definition with parameters that match an invocation exactly. If an exact match is not found, the compiler tries to find a match by promoting integers and converting types where possible (e.g., a double to an int, a derived class pointer to a base class pointer, etc.). If a suitable definition cannot be found, a compilation error occurs. The following rules also apply:

- When considering the parameters of a function, the compiler ignores the presence of `const` or `volatile` and whether a type is a reference type, except when `const` or `volatile` is buried within types. For example, `const int *T` and `int *T` are not treated as distinct, but `int *const T` and `int *T` are (see the discussion of `const` in pointer declarations under "Qualifiers").

- Member functions can be overloaded based on whether they are constant, volatile, or both. The appropriate member function is called based on whether the invoking object is constant or volatile.

- Default arguments make it possible for a single instance of a function to be called using multiple sets of arguments. No overloaded instance of such a function can accept one of those sets of arguments.

Overloading Operators

The operators of C++ have defined behaviors with certain intrinsic types. These behaviors cannot be changed. However, you can define additional behaviors for types of your own. For example, one common practice is to define the `<<` operator so that it can be used with `cout` to display objects of your own class types (see "I/O Streams").

You overload an operator by defining a function called `operatorX`, where `X` is the operator you want to overload. The number of arguments for the function depends on the number of operands an operator requires, and whether you are overloading the operator using a member function or a function that is not a member of a class.

When you overload an operator using a member function, the member function must be nonstatic. The invoking object is the first operand. If the operator requires a second operand, it is passed as an argument to the member function. For example, the following class overloads `+=` in two ways.

```
class Account
{
public:

                     Account(double b)
                     {
                        balance = b;
                     }

      Account        &operator+=(double b)
                     {
                        balance += b;
                        return *this;
                     }

      Account        &operator+=(const
                        Account &a)
                     {
                        balance += a.balance;
                        return *this;
                     }
...
private:
   double          balance;
}
```

Based on the way that the += operator is overloaded in this class, you can do the following:

```
Account        a(50.0);
Account        b(75.0);

a += b;        // a now contains 125.0.
a += 100.0;    // a now contains 225.0.
```

When you overload an operator using a function that is not a member of a class, each operand is passed as an argument. For example:

```
Account &operator+=(Account &a, const
   Account &b)
{
   a.balance += b.balance;
   return a;
}
```

When you use a nonmember function to overload an operator, often you declare it as a friend of its arguments' class types. This is necessary if the function needs to access nonpublic members of its arguments (as shown above).

The following rules also apply:

- The following operators cannot be overloaded: ::, ., .*, ?:, sizeof, typeid, and the C++ cast operators (see "Casts in C++").

- The associativity and precedence of an operator cannot be changed through overloading.

- Derived classes inherit functions that overload operators, except those functions that overload the assignment operator.

- Functions that overload operators cannot have default arguments, except for ( ). This operator can be declared to accept default arguments and can have any number of parameters. Objects of classes that overload the ( ) operator are called *function objects*.

- You can invoke operator functions explicitly (e.g., a. operator+=(b)). If an operator function is a virtual member function and is invoked via a base class pointer or reference, polymorphic behavior occurs.

Assignment operator

Generally, you overload the assignment operator (=) for a class when you define a copy constructor. The assignment operator can be overloaded using a member function only. If you do not overload the assignment operator for a class, member-by-member assignment is performed by default. The function that overloads the assignment operator for a class is not inherited by derived classes.

Memory management operators

The standard header file *<new>* outlines the various ways to overload new, new[], delete, and delete[] (see "Memory Allocation" and "Memory Reclamation"). You can also overload new and new[] for use with placement new. A nonmember function that you provide for overloading a memory management operator does not get called for instances of classes for which you overload the same operator using a member function.

Memory Management

C++ provides intrinsic support for allocating and reclaiming memory dynamically as a program runs. Dynamic memory is memory that you allocate and reclaim (i.e., manage) yourself, as opposed to storage that is managed automatically by the compiler on the stack, for example.

Memory Allocation

The operators used to dynamically allocate memory are new and new[].

new

To dynamically allocate storage for a single instance of a type, you use the new operator. For example:

```
int         *i = new int;
double      *x = new double(10.0);
```

```
Circle              *c = new Circle;
Pt                  *p = new Pt(1.0, 2.0);
```

You provide a comma-delimited list of arguments inside parentheses for initialization, if needed. The result of new is a pointer of the appropriate type.

Initialization takes places after storage is allocated. The number of arguments for initialization must suit the type specified for the allocation. The intrinsic types of C++ take a single argument. The number of arguments and their types for classes depend on the constructors that have been defined by the class. The appropriate constructors are called for an object. Multiple constructors are called if the class of the allocated object is a derived class (see "Constructors and Inheritance").

new[ ]

To dynamically allocate storage for an array, you use the new[ ] operator. For example:

```
double              *da = new double[5];
Circle              *ca = new Circle[8];
```

The class for the objects being allocated must have a default constructor. This constructor is called for each object.

Placement new

Placement new is used to pass additional arguments to a function that overloads new or new[ ]. You can specify any number of arguments that an operator function you have written accepts (see "Overloading Operators"). For example:

```
Account             *a = new(3, x) Account;
```

yields a call like the following:

```
operator new(sizeof(Account), 3, x);
```

The first argument passed to the operator function is the amount of storage to be allocated (specified as a size_t); the remaining arguments are the ones explicitly specified where new is used, in order. Similar rules apply for new[]. For example:

```
Account          *b = new(x) Account[5];
```

yields a call like the following (n is array overhead):

```
operator new[]((sizeof(Account) * 5) + n, x);
```

Failed allocation

If an allocation fails, new and new[] throw a bad_alloc exception. You can use the placement version of new if you prefer a null pointer on a failure:

```
char *c = new(nothrow) char[10];
```

You can install your own handler for dealing with failed allocations by calling set_new_handler (include *<new>*). This function takes a pointer to a handler function with the signature below:

```
void new_handler_function();
```

set_new_handler returns the previously installed handler. If you return from the handler you provide, the allocation is attempted again.

NOTE

I did not use new_handler as the name for my function to deal with failed allocations, because that's a type defined by the standard for new handlers.

Memory Reclamation

The operators used to reclaim dynamically allocated memory are delete and delete[].

delete

To reclaim memory previously allocated using new, you use the delete operator. For example:

```
Circle            *c = new Circle;
...
delete c;
```

The appropriate destructors are called for the object. Multiple destructors may be called if the class of a deleted object is a derived class (see "Destructors and Inheritance").

Once memory has been reclaimed, you must not access it again, although the pointer to it can be pointed to something else. No assumptions can be made about the pointer's value. Using delete with a null pointer is guaranteed to be safe.

WARNING

To ensure that the proper destructors are called, the pointer used with delete must have the same type as the pointer used with new when the memory was allocated, or be a base class pointer.

---

delete[ ]

To reclaim the memory for an array previously allocated using new[ ], you use the delete[ ] operator. For example:

```
Circle            *ca = new Circle[8];
...
delete[] ca;
```

Using delete[], as opposed to delete, causes destructors to be called for each object in an array of objects as memory is reclaimed.

WARNING

As with delete, the pointer used with delete[ ] must have the same type as the pointer used with new[ ] when the memory was allocated, or be a base class pointer.

Casts and Runtime Type Information

Casts are used to explicitly convert an expression's value to a different type. Runtime type information is type data embedded by the compiler for use at runtime.

C-Style Casts

C-style casting is the form of casting inherited from C. The target type is placed in parentheses immediately preceding the expression to be converted, as shown in the assignment to c below:

```
void          *v = new Circle(5.0);
Circle        *c = (Circle *)v;
```

With a C-style cast, no check is performed at runtime to ensure that the cast is reasonable. C-style casting can be used for the following:

- Casting a pointer or arithmetic type to an integer type.
- Casting any arithmetic type to a floating-point type.
- Casting a pointer or arithmetic type to another pointer type.

Casts in C++

C++ provides additional forms of casting, which are generally safer than C-style casts.

dynamic_cast

The dynamic_cast operator casts a pointer of one class type to a pointer of another within a derivation chain. It is allowed only with pointers and references to polymorphic types, which are types that have at least one virtual member function (see "Virtual Member Functions"). For the examples that follow, consider the following derivation chain:

```
class Account
{
   // At least one virtual member
   // function.
};

class BankAccount : virtual public
   Account
{
...
};

class WireAccount : virtual public
   Account
{
...
};

class CheckingAccount : public
   BankAccount, public WireAccount
{
...
};

class SavingsAccount : public
   BankAccount, public WireAccount
{
...
};
```

To use the dynamic_cast operator, you place the target type
inside angle brackets preceding the expression to be
converted; the expression is enclosed in parentheses.

```
Account          *a;
BankAccount      *b;
WireAccount      *w;

CheckingAccount  c;

// Perform an upcast.
a = dynamic_cast<Account *>(&c);

// Do the same thing again to show that
// no cast is required to do an upcast.
a = &c;
```

```
// Perform a downcast.
b = dynamic_cast<BankAccount *>(a);

// Perform a cross cast.
w = dynamic_cast<WireAccount *>(b);
```

This example shows the three operations you are able to perform with the dynamic_cast operator:

upcasting
> The pointer is moved up the derivation chain to a base class.

downcasting
> The pointer is moved down the derivation chain to a derived class.

cross casting
> The pointer is moved to a sibling class within the derivation chain.

NOTE

Since some compilers do not enable runtime type information by default, ensure that runtime type information is turned on for dynamic_cast to work properly.

The following rules also apply to dynamic casts:

- The compiler detects whatever errors it can with dynamic_cast (e.g., a target class type that is not in the derivation chain at all).

- Runtime type information is used to determine whether a cast is legal at runtime. If the cast is determined not to be legal, the result of dynamic_cast is a null pointer. This would be the case in the previous example, for instance, if you were to attempt to downcast an Account pointer to a CheckingAccount pointer when the Account pointer was pointing to a SavingsAccount object.

- When you perform an illegal cast with a reference type, a bad_cast exception is thrown.

---

static_cast

The static_cast operator is used to cast a pointer of one class type to a pointer of another within a derivation chain while avoiding the runtime checks done with dynamic_cast. As a result, you can use the static_cast operator with pointers to nonpolymorphic types, which are types that have no virtual member functions. You also can use it to carry out some of the conversions performed using C-style casts, generally conversions between related types. The static_cast operator has the same syntax as dynamic_cast.

const_cast

You use the const_cast operator to cast away the const and volatile qualifiers. It has the same syntax as dynamic_cast. Between the angle brackets, you specify the same type as the original, without the const or volatile qualifier. Using the result is assured to be safe only if the data to which the pointer points was not declared as const or volatile when it was first declared in the program.

reinterpret_cast

The reinterpret_cast allows you to convert a pointer to any other pointer type. It also allows you to convert any integral type to a pointer and back. It uses a syntax like the other forms of casting specific to C++. It is typically used sparingly.

Runtime Type Information

Runtime type information (RTTI) is type data embedded in a program by the compiler so that you can use it as the program runs. In languages that are statically typed (like C++), type information is normally not available after compilation unless explicitly preserved.

typeid

To get type information about a variable or a type itself, you use the typeid operator. For example:

```
Circle          c(5.0);
const type_info  &t = typeid(c);
```

This assigns information about the type of c to t. The operand for typeid may be an expression or type. The result of the typeid operator is a constant reference to an object of type type_info (see "type_info").

To use the type_info object, you include the standard header file *<typeinfo>*. The following rules apply:

- When the operand for typeid is a reference or a dereferenced pointer to a polymorphic class (a class with at least one virtual member function), the result is type information for the dynamic type of the operand.

- When typeid is applied to a dereferenced null pointer, a bad_typeid exception is thrown.

type_info

The standard type_info class encapsulates support for working with type information. It overloads the == and != operators so that you can easily compare type_info objects. For example:

```
if (typeid(a) == typeid(b))
{
    // a and b have the same type.
}
```

The type_info class also contains a name member function for getting a type's name as a string. The name that is returned is implementation-defined. For example:

```
cout << typeid(c).name() << endl;
```

Exception Handling

Exception handling is performed using try and catch blocks. For example:

```
try
{
    // Watch out for a bad file name
    // or no file handles available.
}
catch (BadFileName &e)
{
    // Handle BadFileName exceptions.
}
catch (HandlesGone &e)
{
    // Handle HandlesGone exceptions.
}
```

try

A try block delineates a context in which exceptions may be raised, or *thrown*. When an exception is thrown within a try block, execution immediately jumps to the start of a catch block responsible for dealing with the exception, if such a block exists.

throw

You throw an exception inside a try block using the throw operator. For example:

```
throw e;
```

The type of the exception is used to determine which catch block to execute. The exception itself is passed as an argument to the catch block so that it can be used in handling the exception. Within a catch block, you can re-throw an exception using throw with no operand. The following rules also apply:

- Exceptions can be of intrinsic types or classes that you define yourself. Exception classes do not have to be derived from any particular class.

- Some standard exceptions are defined for use by the language (e.g., bad_cast thrown by the dynamic_cast operator) and facilities in the C++ Standard Library.

- Standard exceptions are all derived from the exception class, which is defined in the standard header file *<exception>*. The what member function of exception gets a standard exception's name.

catch

One or more catch blocks follow a try block to define how specific types of exceptions should be handled. catch blocks are tried in the order they appear. The first catch block found to match the exception's type or its base class is passed the exception to handle. Therefore, if you catch exceptions of both a derived class and its base class, the catch block for the derived class needs to appear first.

NOTE

Exceptions are often declared as references in catch blocks so that polymorphic behavior is possible when accessing the objects to handle the exceptions.

An ellipsis (...) can be used to indicate that any exception type should be caught. For example:

```
try
{
    // Watch out for a bad file name.
}
catch (BadFileName &e)
```

```
{
    // Handle BadFileName exceptions.
}
catch (...)
{
    // Handle exceptions not covered.
}
```

If no catch block is suitable, the stack is unwound to determine whether a suitable catch block appears earlier in the calling chain. If the stack unwinds completely without finding a suitable catch block, the standard function terminate is called. The default behavior for this function is to terminate the program. You can install your own handler that terminates exception processing by calling set_terminate (include *<exception>*). This function takes a pointer to a handler function with the signature below:

```
void terminate_handler_function();
```

set_terminate returns the previously installed handler. The terminate handler you provide should take any actions necessary for unhandled exceptions, then terminate execution of the program.

Exception Specifications

An exception specification is a guarantee to the caller of a function that only certain exceptions can be thrown within it. For example:

```
void fetch(char *name, char *&data)
    throw (BadFileName, HandlesGone);
```

If the function throws an exception of a type not listed in the exception specification or of a type not derived from one of the listed types, the standard function unexpected is called. The default behavior for this function is to terminate the program. You can install your own handler for this by calling set_unexpected (include *<exception>*). This function takes a pointer to a handler function with the signature below:

```
void unexpected_handler_function();
```

`set_unexpected` returns the previously installed handler. The handler you provide should take any actions necessary for unexpected exceptions, then terminate execution of the program. It can also throw exceptions of its own.

The following rules also apply to exception specifications:

- An empty set of parentheses specifies that a function throws no exceptions.

- If you omit the exception specification altogether, there is no limit on the types or number of exceptions that can be thrown.

- A definition for a function must list the same exceptions as in its declaration.

- If a virtual member function has an exception specification (see "Virtual Member Functions"), the member function of a derived class that overrides the function must have an exception specification that is either the same or more limited than the one in the base class.

The C++ Standard Library

The C++ Standard Library consists of facilities used to perform tasks common to many programs. In addition to facilities specific to C++, such as stream I/O and facilities in the Standard Template Library (STL), the C++ Standard Library provides support for the C Standard Library. To use a feature of the C++ Standard Library, you include the appropriate header file, which contains prototypes, type definitions, and other code required to use certain features.

Header files for the C++ Standard Library do not have a *.h* extension. This enigmatic naming convention was established to avoid compatibility issues with *.h* versions of the header files already in use prior to standardization. Most implementations still provide *.h* (pre-standard) versions of header files for backward compatibility.

The std Namespace

To keep standardized versions of facilities in the C++ Standard Library from conflicting with pre-standard ones, header files without *.h* extensions place their contents within the namespace std. Therefore, to use the standardized facilities, you must qualify them with the std namespace. For example:

```
#include <iostream>
...
std::cout << "Hello" << std::endl;
```

Alternatively, you can use a using directive to alleviate having to specify the namespace. For example:

```
using namespace std;
...
cout << "Hello" << endl;
```

Throughout this reference, a using directive like the one shown here is assumed for examples in which one or more header files from the C++ Standard Library are presumed to have been included.

C Standard Library Support

The C++ Standard Library contains its own versions of standard header files from the C programming language. The names of these header files are similar to their analogs in the C Standard Library; however, they have no *.h* extension and are given the prefix "c" (e.g., *<cstdlib>*). To differentiate the facilities in each header file from their counterparts in the header files of the C Standard Library, each facility is declared in the std namespace. The list below presents the standard header files of C as named in the C++ Standard Library:

<cassert>	*<cctype>*	*<cerrno>*
<cfloat>	*<ciso646>*	*<climits>*
<clocale>	*<cmath>*	*<csetjmp>*
<csignal>	*<cstdarg>*	*<cstddef>*
<cstdio>	*<cstdlib>*	*<cstring>*
<ctime>	*<cwchar>*	*<cwctype>*

C++ Standard Header Files

The C++ Standard Library has facilities for language support, diagnostics, general utilities, strings, locales, containers, iterators, algorithms, numerics, and I/O. The header files for these facilities are listed below. Header files that are part of the Standard Template Library (STL) are marked with an asterisk.

*<algorithm>**	*<bitset>*	*<complex>*
*<deque>**	*<exception>*	*<fstream>*
*<functional>**	*<iomanip>*	*<ios>*
<iosfwd>	*<iostream>*	*<istream>*
*<iterator>**	*<limits>*	*<list>**
<locale>	*<map>**	*<memory>**
<new>	*<numeric>**	*<ostream>*
*<queue>**	*<set>**	*<sstream>*
*<stack>**	*<stdexcept>*	*<streambuf>*
<string>	*<typeinfo>*	*<utility>**
<valarray>	*<vector>**	

I/O Streams

I/O streams are the preferred means of performing input and output via standard I/O and files in C++. Four streams are predefined for standard I/O: cin, cout, cerr, and clog. When writing output, it is common to use the endl manipulator for newlines.

cin

The cin object controls input from a stream buffer associated with the C stream stdin. To use cin, you include the header file *<iostream>*. The type of cin is istream. The istream class overloads the >> operator so that you can use it to read values into variables of intrinsic types. For example:

```
double          value;

cin >> value;
```

You overload the >> operator yourself to read values into objects of types that you define. For example:

```
istream &operator>>(ostream &is,
    Account &a)
{
    return is >> a.balance;
}
```

Assuming this operator function has access to the balance member of Account (usually because you declare such I/O functions as friends of the class), this definition lets you read input directly into Account objects. For example:

```
Account          account;

cin >> account;
```

Because the operator function returns a reference to the istream object passed to the function, you can chain input operations together. For example:

```
Account          a1, a2;

cin >> a1 >> a2;
```

The wcin object is the analog to cin for working with wide-character streams (see "char and wchar_t").

cout

The cout object controls output to a stream buffer associated with the C stream stdout. To use cout, you include the header file *<iostream>*. The type of cout is ostream. The ostream class overloads the << operator so that you can use it to write variables of intrinsic types as output. For example:

```
char             s[] = "Hello";

cout << s << endl;
```

You overload the << operator yourself to write out objects of types that you define. For example:

```
ostream &operator<<(ostream &os, const
    Account &a)
```

```
{
    return os << a.balance;
}
```

Assuming this operator function has access to the balance member of Account (usually because you declare such I/O functions as friends of the class), this definition lets you write Account objects directly as output. For example:

```
Account          account;
...
cout << account << endl;
```

Because the operator function returns a reference to the ostream object passed to the function, you can chain output operations together. For example:

```
Account          a1, a2;
...
cout << a1 << ", " << a2 << endl;
```

The wcout object is the analog to cout for working with wide-character streams (see "char and wchar_t").

cerr

The cerr object controls output to a stream buffer associated with the C stream stderr. To use cerr, you include the header file *<iostream>*. Aside from working with stderr, which is unbuffered, the mechanics of cerr are similar to those described previously for cout. The wcerr object is the analog to cerr for working with wide-character streams (see "char and wchar_t").

clog

Like cerr, the clog object controls output to a stream buffer associated with the C stream stderr; however, output is buffered. To use clog, you include the header file *<iostream>*. The wclog object is the analog to clog for working with wide-character streams (see "char and wchar_t").

Index

Symbols

-- (postfix decrement
    operator), 39
-- (prefix decrement
    operator), 40
- (subtraction operator), 41
! (logical NOT operator), 40
!= operator, 43
& (address-of operator), 41
& (bitwise AND operator), 43
&& (logical AND operator), 44
( ) (value construction
    operator), 39
* (indirection operator), 41
+ (plus operator), 41
++ (postfix increment
    operator), 39
++ (prefix increment
    operator), 40
. (member selection
    operator), 38
.* operator, 42
:: (scope resolution operator), 37
:? (conditional expression
    operator), 45
< operator, 43

<< (left shift operator), 43
<= operator, 43
<climits> header file, 13
== operator, 43
-> (member selection
    operator), 38
> operator, 43
->* operator, 42
>= operator, 43
>> (right shift operator), 43
[ ] (array subscript operator), 38
\ (backslash), 8
^ (bitwise XOR operator), 43
| (bitwise OR operator), 43
|| (logical OR operator), 44
~ (bitwise NOT operator), 40

A

abstract base classes, 94
access levels for members, 78
access specifiers, 78
addition operator (+), 42
address-of operator (&), 41
arithmetic operators, 42
array subscript operator ([ ]), 38

We'd like to hear your suggestions for improving our indexes. Send email to
index@oreilly.com.

arrays, 19–22
  initializer list for, 21
  initializing with an array, 22
  multidimensional, 20
  passing to functions, 21
assignment operators, 34, 45
  overloading, 107
atof( ) function, 5
auto storage class, 56

B

backslash (\), 8
base classes, 89
  virtual, 97
bitwise AND operator (&), 43
bitwise NOT operator (~), 40
bitwise OR operator (|), 43
bitwise XOR operator (^), 43
break statement, 64

C

C Standard Library, 121
C++ programs
  startup, 3–5
  structure, 3–12
  termination, 5
C++ Standard Library, 120–124
C, compatibility with, 2
catch blocks, 118
cerr object, 124
character escape sequences, 14
character literals, 14
cin object, 122
class scope, 47
class types, 28
classes, 69–86
  storage, 55–56
clog object, 124
clone member function, 108
comments, 32
compound statements, 59
compound types, 17–28

conditional expression operator
      (:?), 45
const qualifier, 57
const_cast operator, 39, 115
constant data members, 72
constant member functions, 77
constructors, 80–83
  converting, 30
  copy, 81
  default, 81
  explicit, 82
  inheritance and, 89
  member initializers, 83
continue statement, 64
copy constructors, 81
cout object, 123
_ _cplusplus macro, 12
.cpp files, 7
cross casting, 114
C-style cast operator, 42
C-style casting, 112

D

data members
  constant, 72
  declaring, 70–73
  mutable, 73
  static, 71
  volatile, 73
_ _DATE_ _ macro, 11
declarations, 50–58
  forward, 86
  nested, 85
default arguments, 53
#define directive, 6, 8
delete operator, 42, 110
delete[ ] operator, 42, 111
dereferencing pointers, 24, 41
derived classes, 89
destructors, 83
  inheritance and, 90
  virtual, 90
directives, preprocessor, 8–11

division operator (/), 42
do loop, 60
double type, 16
downcasting, 114
dynamic_cast operator, 39,
        112–114

E

#elif directive, 9
ellipsis (...) and exception
        handling, 118
#else directive, 9
enclosing scopes, 49
#endif directive, 6, 9
enum keyword, 18
enumerations, 18
#error directive, 10
escape sequences, 14
exception handling, 117–120
    ellipsis (...) and, 118
exception specifications, 119
exit function, 5
explicit specialization
    of template classes, 100
    of template functions, 102
expression statements, 59
expressions, 46
extern storage class, 56

F

file scope, 48
_ _FILE_ _ macro, 11
float type, 16
floating points, 16
for loops, 61
    break statements and, 64
forward declarations, 86
friends, 79
function call operator, 38
function pointers, 25

functions
    declaring, 52
    definitions, 53
    inline, 54
    overloading, 104
    parameters, 53
    passing arrays to, 21
fundamental types, 12–17

G

global namespaces, 66
goto statement, 65

H

header files, 5–7
    C++ Standard Library, 120
    wrapping, 6

I

I/O streams, 122
identifiers, 32
    rules, 33
#if directive, 9
if statement, 62
#ifdef directive, 9
#ifndef directive, 6, 9
implicit conversions, 29
#include directive, 6, 10
indirection operator (*), 41
inheritance, 88–98
    access levels for, 94
    constructors and, 89
    destructors and, 90
    multiple, 95
initializer list for arrays, 21
inline functions, 54
inline keyword, 54
int type, 15
integers, 15
iteration statements, 60–62

J

jump statements, 64

L

left shift operator (<<), 43
#line directive, 10
__LINE__ macro, 11
literals, 34
local scope, 47
logical AND operator (&&), 44
logical NOT operator (!), 40
logical OR operator (||), 44
long double type, 16
long type, 15
loops, 60–62
l-values, 28
  references as, 28

M

main( ) function, 3
member access levels, 78
member functions, 74–78
  constant, 77
  static, 76
  this pointer and, 75
  virtual, 91–94
  volatile, 78
member functions and volatile
      qualifiers, 58
member initializers, 82
member selection operator
    (. and ->), 38
memory allocation failure, 110
memory management, 108–111
  operators, 108
memory reclamation, 110
message directive, 11
minus operator (-), 41
modulus operator (%), 42
multidimensional arrays, 20
multiple inheritance, 95
multiplication operator (*), 42

mutable data members, 73
mutable storage class, 56

N

namespace scope, 48
namespaces, 66–68
  global, 66
  unnamed, 68
nested declarations, 85
new operator, 42, 108
new[ ] operator, 42, 109
null pointers, 25
null statements, 59

O

.o files, 7
.obj files, 7
objects
  accessing members, 69
  declaring, 69
operators, 34–46
  list of, 35–37
  overloading, 105–108
  precedence, 35
overloading
  defined, 104
  functions, 104
  operators, 105–108

P

parameters, function, 53
plus operator (+), 41
pointer arithmetic, 24
pointer variables, 51
pointers, 24–27
  const declaration, 57
  dereferencing, 24, 41
  function, 25
  null, 25
  of type void, 25
  this, 75

pointers to members, 26
pointer-to-member selection
        operators (.* and –>*), 42
postfix increment and decrement
        operators (++, --), 39
#pragma directive, 11
precedence, operator, 35
prefix increment and decrement
        operators, 40
preprocessor directives, 8–11
preprocessor macros, 11
private members, 78
    inheritance and, 95
protected members, 78
    inheritance and, 95
prototypes, 53
public members, 78
    inheritance and, 95

Q

qualifiers, 57

R

reference parameters, 27
references, 27
    as l-values, 28
register storage class, 56
reinterpret_cast operator, 39,
        115
relational operators, 43
reserved words, 33
return statement, 65
right shift operator (>>), 43
RTTI (runtime type
        information), 115

S

scope resolution operator (::), 37
scopes, 47–50
    class, 47
    enclosing, 49

file, 48
    local, 47
    namespace, 48
selection statements, 62
sequence operator (,), 46
set_new_handler function, 110
set_terminate function, 119
shift operators, 43
short type, 15
signed integers, 15
sizeof operator, 40
source files, 7
Standard Template Library
        (STL), 122
statements, 59–65
static data members, 71
static member functions, 76
static storage class, 55
static_cast operator, 39, 115
std namespace, 121
_ _STDC_ _ macro, 12
STL (Standard Template
        Library), 122
storage classes, 55–56
string literals, 23
strings, 22
strlen function, 23
structs, 86
subtraction operator (-), 42
switch statement, 63

T

template classes, 98–101
    default arguments for, 101
    explicit specialization of, 100
    member functions in, 99
    nontype parameters in, 100
template functions, 101–103
    arguments to, 102
    explicit specialization of, 102
    instantiation of, 102
    nontype parameters in, 103
templates, 98–103

this pointer, 75
throw operator, 46, 117
_ _TIME_ _ macro, 11
_ _TIMESTAMP_ _ macro, 11
tokens, 31
try block, 117
type cast operators, 39
type conversions, 28–30
type definitions, 31
type_info class, 116
typedef keyword, 28, 31
typeid operator, 39, 116
types
  compound, 17–28
  fundamental, 12–17

U

unary minus and plus operators
  (-, +), 41
#undef directive, 9
unexpected function, 119
unions, 86
unnamed namespaces, 68
unsigned integers, 15
upcasting, 114
user-defined conversions, 29
using declaration, 67
using directives, 67

V

value construction operator, 39
variables
  declarations, 51
  initializing, 52
virtual base classes, 97
virtual destructors, 90
virtual member functions, 91–94
void pointers, 25
void type, 17
volatile data members, 73
volatile member functions, 78
volatile qualifier, 58
  member functions and, 58

W

while loop, 60
wide characters, 23
wrapping header files, 6

Need in-depth answers fast?

Access over 2,000 of the newest and best technology books online

Safari Bookshelf is the premier electronic reference library for IT professionals and programmers—a must-have when you need to pinpoint exact answers in an instant.

Access over 2,000 of the top technical reference books by twelve leading publishers including O'Reilly, Addison-Wesley, Peachpit Press, Prentice Hall, and Microsoft Press. Safari provides the technical references and code samples you need to develop quality, timely solutions.

Try it today with a FREE TRIAL
Visit *www.oreilly.com/safari/max*

For groups of five or more, set up a free, 30-day corporate trial
Contact: *corporate@oreilly.com*

What Safari Subscribers Say:

"The online books make quick research a snap. I usually keep Safari up all day and refer to it whenever I need it."

—Joe Bennett, Sr. Internet Developer

"I love how Safari allows me to access new books each month depending on my needs. The search facility is excellent and the presentation is top notch. It is one heck of an online technical library."

—Eric Winslow, Economist-System,
Administrator-Web Master-Programmer

Related Titles Available from O'Reilly

C and C++ Programming

C Pocket Reference

C++ in a Nutshell

C++: The Core Language

Mastering Algorithms with C

Objective-C Pocket Reference

Practical C Programming, *3rd Edition*

Practical C++ Programming, *2nd Edition*

Programming Embedded Systems
in C and C++

Secure Programming Cookbook
for C and C++

STL Pocket Reference

O'REILLY®

Our books are available at most retail and online bookstores.
To order direct: 1-800-998-9938 • *order@oreilly.com* • *www.oreilly.com*
Online editions of most O'Reilly titles are available at *safari.oreilly.com*

Keep in touch with O'Reilly

1. Download examples from our books

To find example files for a book, go to:
www.oreilly.com/catalog

select the book, and follow the "Examples" link.

2. Register your O'Reilly books

Register your book at *register.oreilly.com*

Why register your books? Once you've registered your O'Reilly books you can:

- Win O'Reilly books, T-shirts or discount coupons in our monthly drawing.
- Get special offers available only to registered O'Reilly customers.
- Get catalogs announcing new books (US and UK only).
- Get email notification of new editions of the O'Reilly books you own.

3. Join our email lists

Sign up to get topic-specific email announcements of new books and conferences, special offers, and O'Reilly Network technology newsletters at:
elists.oreilly.com

It's easy to customize your free elists subscription so you'll get exactly the O'Reilly news you want.

4. Get the latest news, tips, and tools

www.oreilly.com

- "Top 100 Sites on the Web"—PC Magazine
- CIO Magazine's Web Business 50 Awards

Our web site contains a library of comprehensive product information (including book excerpts and tables of contents), downloadable software, background articles, interviews with technology leaders, links to relevant sites, book cover art, and more.

5. Work for O'Reilly

Check out our web site for current employment opportunities:
jobs.oreilly.com

6. Contact us

O'Reilly & Associates
1005 Gravenstein Hwy North
Sebastopol, CA 95472 USA

TEL: 707-827-7000 or 800-998-9938
     (6am to 5pm PST)

FAX: 707-829-0104

order@oreilly.com
> For answers to problems regarding your order or our products.
> To place a book order online, visit:
> *www.oreilly.com/order_new*

catalog@oreilly.com
> To request a copy of our latest catalog.

booktech@oreilly.com
> For book content technical questions or corrections.

corporate@oreilly.com
> For educational, library, government, and corporate sales.

proposals@oreilly.com
> To submit new book proposals to our editors and product managers.

international@oreilly.com
> For information about our international distributors or translation queries.
> For a list of our distributors outside of North America check out:
> *international.oreilly.com/distributors.html*

adoption@oreilly.com
> For information about academic use of O'Reilly books, visit:
> *academic.oreilly.com*

O'REILLY®

Our books are available at most retail and online bookstores.
To order direct: 1-800-998-9938 • *order@oreilly.com* • *www.oreilly.com*
Online editions of most O'Reilly titles are available at *safari.oreilly.com*